Introduction

The **Clwydian Range**, designated as an *Area of ̫ ̫ding Natural Beauty*, is a chain of undulating hills, runr ̫ ̫ ̫ ̫ ̫ ̫ the Vale of Clwyd and the Dee Estuary in North Wa ̫ ̫ ̫ ̫ ̫ 22 miles from Prestatyn and the coast, risinɡ ̫ ̫ ̫ ̫ ̫ft, before descending to Nant y Garth, ρ ̫ ̫ ̫ ̫ ̫ ̫ ̫ miles. Within the AONB are **Logɡ ̫ ̫ ̫ ̫ ̫ ̫ ̫ ̫ ̫ ̫ ̫ ırks** – the latter, with its imprɛ ̫ ̫ ̫ ̫ ̫ ̫ ̫ ̫ ̫ ̫ ̫ ̫ e of the largest in Wales.

The Range provides a diν ̫ ̫ ̫ ̫ ̫ ̫ ̫ ̫ ̫ ̫ ındscape scenery, including heather-clad moorla ̫ ̫ ̫ ̫ ̫ ̫ ̫ ̫ ̫ıells, limestone crags, woodland, river valleys, ano ̫ ̫ ̫ ̫ ̫ ̫ımland. In addition, the Clwydians contain many importa ̫ ̫ ̫ ̫ ̫ ɔtorical and archaeological sites dating from the time of early man to the industrial age. Particularly impressive are the remains of six iron-age hill forts. Running through the full length of the Range is one of the most scenic sections of **Offa's Dyke Path** – a 177 mile National Trail from the Severn in South Wales to Prestatyn in the North.

The Clwydian Range is a wonderful walking area, offering panoramic views, but many parts of it are still little known. This book explores its diverse scenery and rich heritage through 15 linked circular walks based on Offa's Dyke Path. The routes, which range from 4 to 6½ miles, follow public rights of way or permissive paths, and are well within the capabilities of most walkers. *A key feature is that individual walks can easily be linked, in various combinations, to provide longer and more challenging day walks if required.* Walking boots or strong shoes are recommended, along with appropriate clothing to protect against the elements. Please remember that the condition of the paths can vary according to season and weather!

Each walk has a detailed map and description which enables the route to be followed without difficulty, but be aware that changes in detail can occur *at any time*. The location of each walk is shown on the back cover and a summary of the key characteristics of each is also given. This includes an estimated walking time, but the scenery is far too good to hurry through, so allow more time for its enjoyment. Whilst the starting points reflect the use of a car, the majority of walks are accessible by public transport. Further details can be obtained by calling 01824 706968.

Please observe the country code and take particular care not to damage any of the ancient sites visited. Finally, I wish to thank the staff of Denbighshire Countryside Service and the Public Rights of Way Officer for their advice and assistance. *Enjoy your walking!*

Walk 1
GRAIG FAWR AND COED YR ESGOB

DESCRIPTION This easy 4-mile walk provides a fascinating exploration of the low limestone hills above Dyserth and Meliden at the northern end of the Clwydian Range. It takes you to the magnificent viewpoint of Graig Fawr, owned by the National Trust, through an ancient oak wood, and returns along a disused railway line – now a pleasant recreational walkway. It is an area rich in industrial archaelogy. Allow about 2½ hours.
START Lay-by on A5151 on the outskirts of Dyserth. SJ 066795.
DIRECTIONS From Rhuddlan take the A5151, passing through the centre of Dyserth. Park in a lay-by next to a telephone box on the left, half-way up a hill when leaving Dyserth on the way to Trelawnyd.

1 Take the lane by the lay-by, and then the right track ahead, to cross a stile alongside *The Glen*. Now follow a rough track until it swings right by a gate to end in a field. Follow the field boundary on the left to a stile and continue ahead to reach a road, where you turn LEFT to a T-junction. Cross half-LEFT to a car park and access to Graig Fawr. *Graig Fawr is a notable limestone hill owned by the National Trust and managed as a local amenity. It is a Site of Special Scientific Interest and an important area for nature conservation.*

2 From the kissing-gate, a path heading half-LEFT will take you to the trig point on the summit. *This offers panoramic views of the North Wales coast and the mountains of Snowdonia. Nearer, looking towards the south-west, are the remains of the Clive Engine House, a scheduled monument, built in the 1860s to house a massive steam engine which pumped water from the Talargoch lead and zinc mines. The main shaft was 1000' deep, but the high cost of keeping the mine dry led to its closure in 1884.* From the trig point head south-east towards a large house to reach a kissing-gate and a road, where you turn LEFT.

3 On reaching *Laburnum Cottage (one of several cottages built by miners on common land)* turn LEFT and then RIGHT onto Offa's Dyke Path. The path takes you down a drive, and then passes to the right of *Red Roofs* to soon reach the open gorse-clad hillside with fine views. *Imagine what it feels like as a long distance walker when ahead lies Prestatyn, the sea, and the finish of a two-week trek from South Wales!* The path then swings right through a kissing-gate to enter a small wood. Follow the Acorn signs (Prestatyn), passing two path junctions, soon to walk along the rim of a disused quarry. *Large quantities of limestone have been extracted from local quarries over centuries, primarily to produce lime for the chemical industry, for use in steel making, and as a fertilizer.*

4 At a waymark post leave Offa's Dyke Path to head LEFT down to Coed yr Esgob (Bishop's Wood). The path winds its way steadily down through an area of predominantly oak woodland, passing the entrance to the *Fish Mine* to reach the bottom of the wood. *Coed yr Esgob is an area of unspoilt natural woodland which is designated as a Site of Special Scientific Interest. It provides a rich haven for plants, animals and birds. The calcite and lead mine, which closed at the beginning of the 20thC, was allegedly named because its spoil tip resembled the shape of a fish. Another possible explanation might be the presence of fossilised fish in the limestone.* Follow a path LEFT along the edge of the wood, to reach a lane. Cross the stile on your right and go down the field to join a disused railway line. *This is the former Prestatyn – Dyserth branch railway, which was opened by the London & North Western Railway in 1869 to serve the local mines and quarries. A passsenger service ran between 1905 and 1930, and the line was eventually*

WALK 1

closed in 1973. On this route look for the gallows-like remains of a loading gauge, used to ensure that wagons could pass safely under bridges or station roofs.

5 Follow the old line LEFT, passing beneath Graig Fawr, through attractive woodland, and under two fine stone and brick bridges. *Before reaching the first bridge look for a disused quarry on your left. The top of this hill is the site of Dyserth Castle, built by Henry III in 1241 and destroyed in 1263 by Llewelyn ap Gruffydd, the last of the native Welsh princes. Few remains now survive.* When the walkway passes over a river, turn LEFT on a path to the road, which you follow LEFT back to the start. *This walk can be linked to* **Walk 2** *by taking a path on the right as you go up the road. Before leaving the area, visits to Dyserth Waterfall and the Church of St. Bridget and St. Cwyfan, with its fine medieval stained glass window, are highly recommended.*

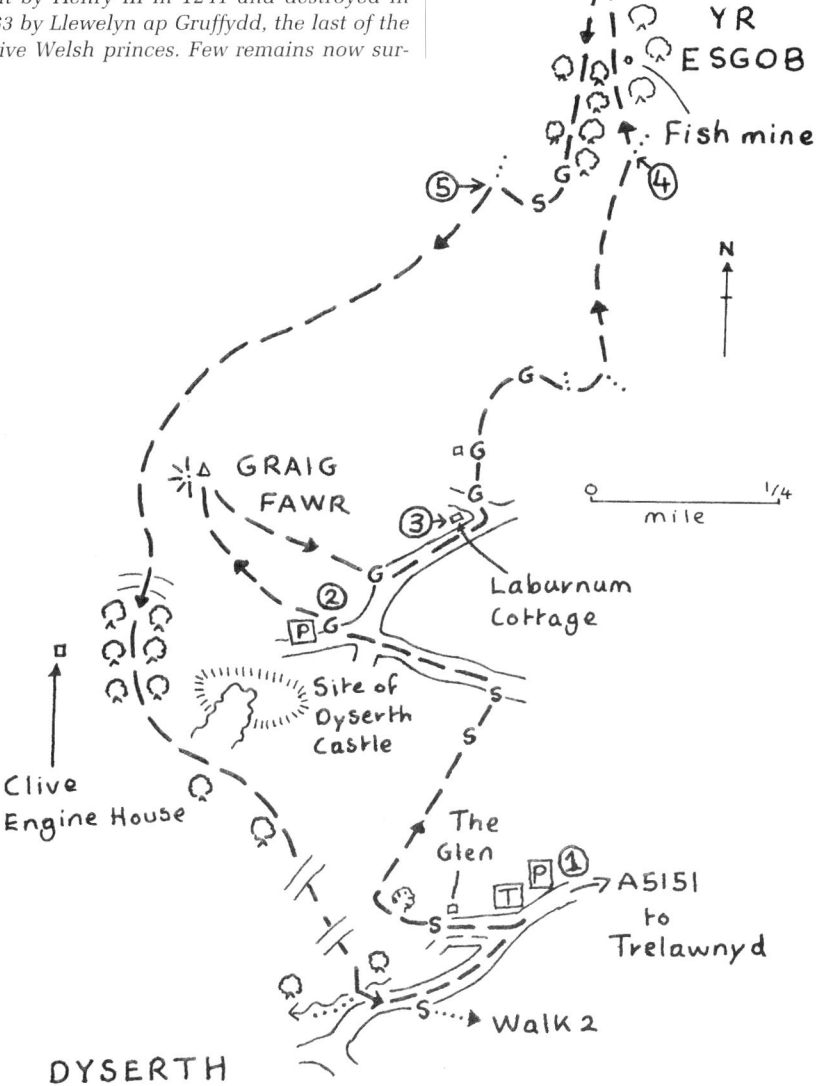

Walk 2

MARION FRITH, CWM AND MOEL HIRADDUG

DESCRIPTION An enjoyable 5-mile ramble across open, undulating countryside to the top of a small limestone hill offering fine views, then down to the village of Cwm and its 17thC inn. The route, which follows mainly field and woodland paths, takes in a disused railway line, passes two old water-mills, and skirts an iron-age fort. Allow about 3 hours.

START Lay-by on A5151 on the outskirts of Dyserth. SJ 066795.
DIRECTIONS From Rhuddlan take the A5151, passing through the centre of Dyserth. Park in a lay-by next to a telephone box on the left, half-way up a hill out of Dyserth on the way to Trelawnyd.

1 Head back down the road to take a path on the left by a stile/gate alongside a water treatment works. A waymarked path follows the course of an old railway line to reach a minor road. *In 1884, H D Pochin, a local landowner, built at his own expense, the first ¾ mile of a proposed extension of the Prestatyn -Dyserth railway to the nearby village of Trelawynd. It was never completed beyond Marion Mill.* Follow the road LEFT past the remains of Grove Mill and on to take the Offa's Dyke Path (Cwm) along a stone track ahead to Marion Mill. *The fast flowing stream once turned the water-wheels of these mills, generating power for turning corn into flour and for the fulling process in the preparation of yarns and woven fabric.*

2 Here follow Offa's Dyke Path RIGHT along an enclosed green track, and then LEFT over a stile to cross two fields and a road, to go along a green track. The path turns left over a stile to cross two fields to reach a track which you follow LEFT, passing a farm to cross a stile on your right.

3 The path now heads up, over a stile, to rise steadily slightly left to pass over the open pasture of Marian Ffrith. *The pleasant hilltop of Marian Ffrith offers good views of two ancient historical sites. To the north-east is the distinctive dome of Gop Hill, the largest prehistoric burial cairn in Wales. To the north-west is Moel Hiraddug, the most northerly of the Clwydian iron-age hillforts, sadly ravaged by quarrying. In the 19thC, part of a 2ndC BC ceremonial shield was found here.* Marker posts lead you down to cross a road at the tiny hamlet of Marian Cwm. The path passes by a cottage and on up a large field, swinging left to a stile, over a road and up a field to turn LEFT at another road.

4 Leave Offa's Dyke Path by taking a path on your right up a green track by a wood, soon swinging right to cross a stile by a ruin. Follow the fence on your left, passing a derelict building, and on down through a section of mixed woodland, turning RIGHT at a marker post down to a road. *As you descend the hillside enjoy the fine views across the deep wooded valley to Cwm and the dominant end of Moel Hiraddug.* Continue ahead to turn LEFT down another road into Cwm. *The Church of St. Mael and St. Sulien is worth a visit, and you can enjoy some refreshment at the Blue Lion Inn.*

5 Continue, passing the inn to cross a stile on the right by a cottage, and on to turn LEFT by a wood. Go over a stile, continue up the field ahead and then down to cross a road and over a stile. The path now heads half-LEFT around the base of Moel Hiraddug, soon dropping gently down through a delightful area of woodland to reach a lane, which joins a road leading into Dyserth.

WALK 2

6 Soon head half-RIGHT up Upper Foel Road, passing several disused lime kilns on your right, and carry on to reach the main road. *Limestone from the huge quarry on medieval stained glass window, are highly recommended.*

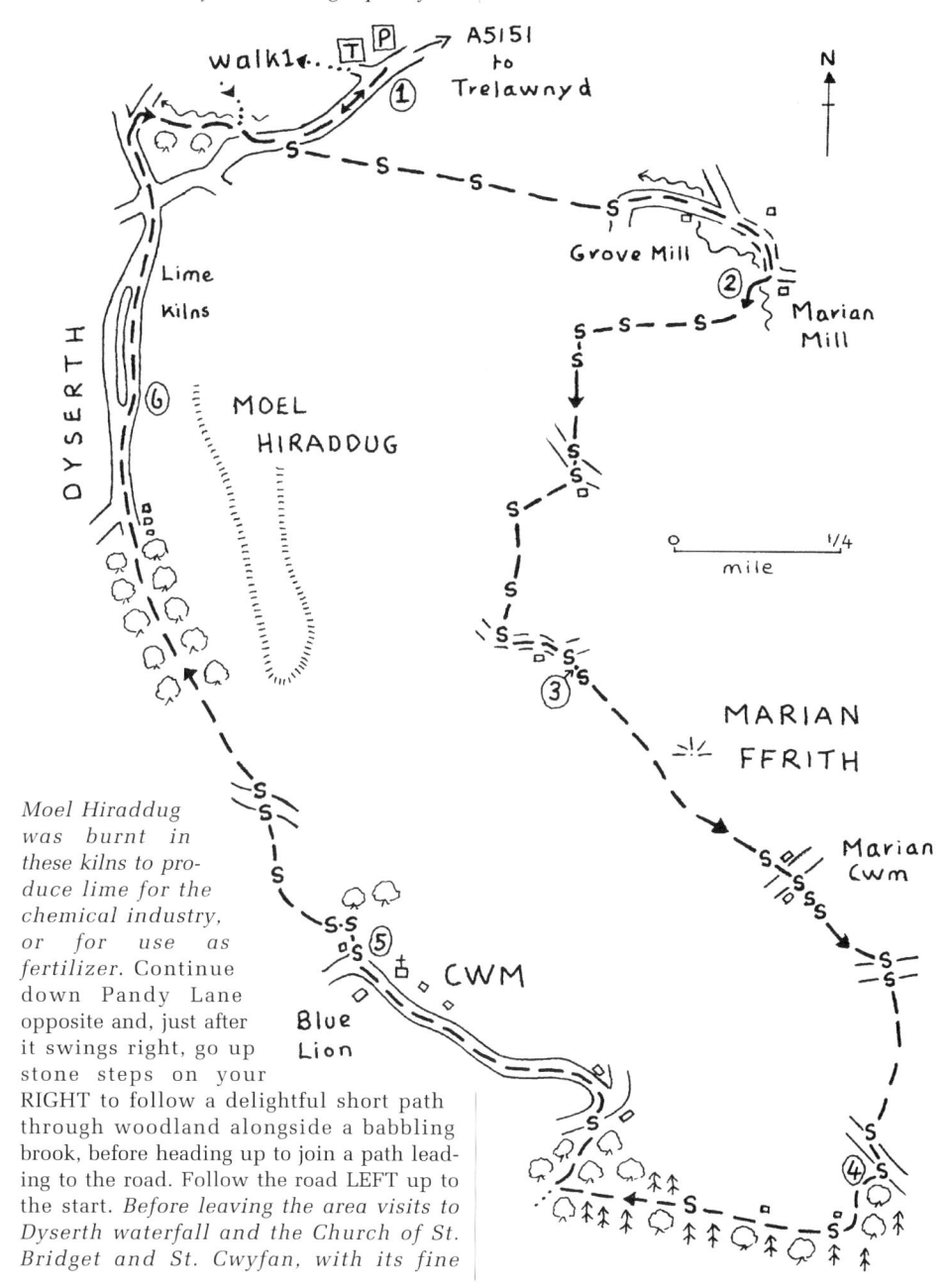

Moel Hiraddug was burnt in these kilns to produce lime for the chemical industry, or for use as fertilizer. Continue down Pandy Lane opposite and, just after it swings right, go up stone steps on your RIGHT to follow a delightful short path through woodland alongside a babbling brook, before heading up to join a path leading to the road. Follow the road LEFT up to the start. *Before leaving the area visits to Dyserth waterfall and the Church of St. Bridget and St. Cwyfan, with its fine*

Walk 3

TREMEIRCHION AND Y GRAIG

DESCRIPTION A splendid 4½ mile walk over undulating countryside, offering panoramic views and sites of historic and scenic interest. The route starts from a medieval church, passes near a 19thC Jesuit College, takes you through a little known nature reserve, and finally near caves once occupied by stone age man. The walk follows clear paths and bridleways and quiet country lanes. Allow about 3 hours.
START Church of Corpus Christi, Tremeirchion. SJ 083731.
DIRECTIONS From Bodfari take the B5429 towards Tremeirchion. After about 2 miles, by Brynbella, take a right turn, and then soon fork up right to park alongside the church.

Before starting the walk, visit the attractive Church of Corpus Christi, which dates mainly from the 14th and 15thC. Items to see include a 13thC cross slab forming a seat in the porch, rare 17thC portrait glass, an impressive canopied 14thC tomb, and many other ancient features (more details are available in the church). A yew tree outside is reputed to be over 800 years old.

1 From the church walk up the road past *The Salusbury Arms* – a 14thC coaching inn – to take a waymarked path on the left through a gate. Head straight across the field, over a stile and then half-RIGHT over another. Continue half-RIGHT across two fields and down to cross a stile in the field corner. Walk up the field ahead, close to the field boundary on the right. *Prominent on the skyline, rising out of the trees on the left, is the church of St. Beuno's College. The College was built in 1848 as an institution for theological students and many Jesuit priests received their final training there. The renowned poet Gerard Manley Hopkins studied at the College from 1874-77, and was ordained in the chapel. It was here he wrote some of his major poems. The College is now a retreat for those who wish to meditate.*

2 When the boundary swings right, head down the field to cross a stream in the field corner, and on over a stile to pass across the front of *Ysgubor* to reach a lane. Turn RIGHT and, after about 80 yards, go over a partly-hidden stile on the left. Head over to the fence beyond a house, and follow this round to the left to cross two stiles in quick succession. Follow the field boundary on the left to cross a stile in it, just beyond the last patch of gorse. Take the woodland path, soon dropping down to a lane, which you follow to the RIGHT.

3 Take the waymarked Offa's Dyke Path behind *Benarth*. It soon leaves a bridleway, rising steadily to reach a prominent marker post by two hawthorn trees. *This spot offers tremendous views of the Vale of Clwyd, the North Wales coast, and the distant mountains of Snowdonia. A good place to linger for a while.* The path now crosses two fields, and then passes a small caravan site to reach a road, which you follow to the RIGHT, down to a T-junction. Turn LEFT, then take the next road RIGHT and, when it turns sharp left, cross the stile ahead.

4 Offa's Dyke Path continues up the field, but this route follows a green track, swinging right alongside a fence, and then half-left, as the fence begins to descend, to reach a gate surrounded by gorse. Continue with this delightful green track as it gently meanders down into the valley ahead, and on through two gates, passing a farm entrance and then on to reach a road. Go ahead for 50 yards.

5 Turn RIGHT along a driveway waymarked *Tremeirchion/Y Graig* and, when it swings right, take a narrow path ahead to enter Y Graig Nature Reserve. *Y Graig is a prominent limestone crag, which was bought by The North Wales Wildlife Trust with local support in 1987. The ancient woodland and grassland, which has apparently never been occupied by man, supports a wide range of wildlife and plants.* Follow the path to the

WALK 3

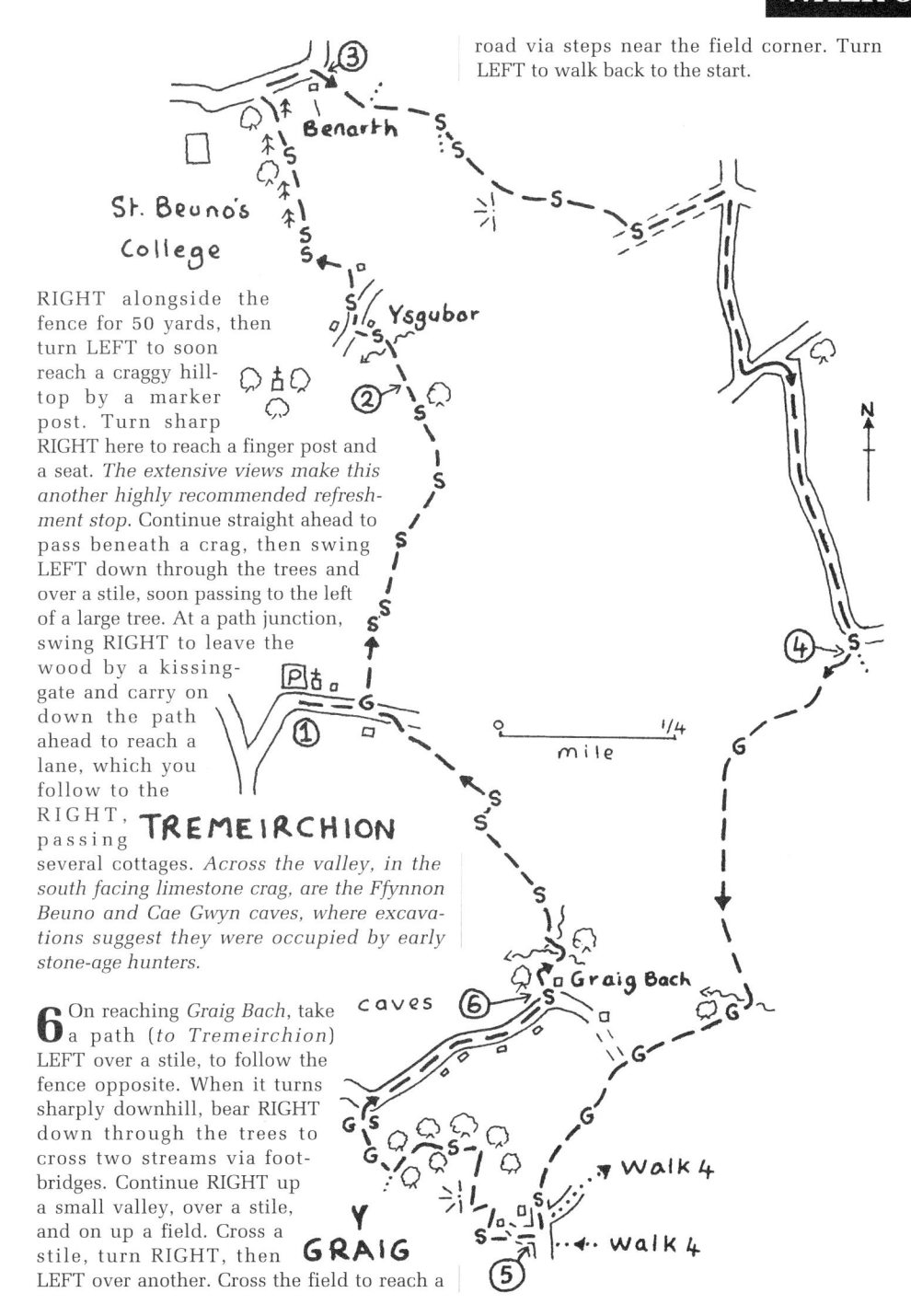

road via steps near the field corner. Turn LEFT to walk back to the start.

RIGHT alongside the fence for 50 yards, then turn LEFT to soon reach a craggy hilltop by a marker post. Turn sharp RIGHT here to reach a finger post and a seat. *The extensive views make this another highly recommended refreshment stop.* Continue straight ahead to pass beneath a crag, then swing LEFT down through the trees and over a stile, soon passing to the left of a large tree. At a path junction, swing RIGHT to leave the wood by a kissing-gate and carry on down the path ahead to reach a lane, which you follow to the RIGHT, passing several cottages. *Across the valley, in the south facing limestone crag, are the Ffynnon Beuno and Cae Gwyn caves, where excavations suggest they were occupied by early stone-age hunters.*

6 On reaching *Graig Bach*, take a path (*to Tremeirchion*) LEFT over a stile, to follow the fence opposite. When it turns sharply downhill, bear RIGHT down through the trees to cross two streams via footbridges. Continue RIGHT up a small valley, over a stile, and on up a field. Cross a stile, turn RIGHT, then LEFT over another. Cross the field to reach a

Walk 4

MOEL-Y-GAER AND SODOM

DESCRIPTION This figure-of-eight 4½-mile walk explores attractive undulating countryside north of Bodfari, following clear paths, old green tracks and quiet country roads. Highlights include an iron-age fort, panoramic views, the opportunity to enjoy traditional Welsh home-cooking, an optional visit to Y Graig nature reserve, and an old inn at the finish. Sodom is notable for its views – and its name! Apart from an early short steep section, walking is easy. Allow about 3 hours

START Dinorben Arms, Bodfari. SJ 093701

DIRECTIONS Take the A541 Denbigh-Mold road to Bodfari, then turn off on the B5429 towards Tremeirchion, to reach the Dinorben Arms inn, next to the church. Permission has kindly been granted for parking in the bottom car park.

Bodfari, possibly the site of a Roman way-station, was once famous for St. Deifar's holy well, where it was the custom to dip children three times to prevent their crying at night.

1 Leave the car park by its exit and turn LEFT along the road. Then take a waymarked path LEFT passing the old school, and continue by a children's play area and some bungalows to reach a road. Turn LEFT here and follow the narrowing road uphill, soon swinging right. Just after the first house, cross a stile on the LEFT and head uphill towards a marker post. *You are now on Offa's Dyke Path. Follow the path round the edge of the field and up to reach a stile. Pause to enjoy the fine views looking south down the Vale of Clwyd to the Llantisilio Mountains, Moel Famau with its ruined tower, and closer to Moel-y-Parc, with its TV transmitter mast, which dominates the Wheeler Valley.*

2 Go over the stile. The path beneath Moel y Gaer soon swings LEFT uphill through trees as you approach farm buildings, then drops half-RIGHT down to cross a stile onto a farm drive. Head half-LEFT down the field to cross a stile onto a lane. Turn LEFT, and then fork LEFT off the lane to a second finger post.

3 Here you leave Offa's Dyke Path, by going half-RIGHT on a delightful path through the trees on what used to be an old road, to reach a lane, which you follow LEFT past corrugated sheds, to reach a junction. Take the minor road RIGHT to pass *Fron-Haul*, before swinging sharp LEFT on a road passing behind the house. *Fron Haul is a farmhouse which welcomes walkers, offering coffee, lunches and afternoon teas. On a fine day it is extremely pleasant to sit in the garden enjoying home baking, whilst taking in the views!*

4 At a crossroads, continue ahead on a quiet attractive country road, passing an old water trough, and a converted chapel. *There are fine views over the Vale of Clwyd towards the mountains of Snowdonia.* Where the road swings down to the left, go ahead on a path through the woods and on over a field to reach a lane.

5 Here you can link into **Walk 3**. *A short diversion of about ¼-mile there-and-back will take you to the splendid summit of Y Graig Nature Reserve.* Your main route continues by turning RIGHT on the lane, which then swings right to end by a house. The path continues up a delightful green track, which soon winds its way up the edge of a valley, in tranquil open country, to reach a road, where you rejoin the Offa's Dyke Path. Follow the road RIGHT for half-a-mile to pass through the cross-roads met at point **4**, and on to turn RIGHT at a T-junction. *This section of attractive, quiet country road will surprise you with its sudden panoramic views.*

6 Cross a stile on the left. *This is perhaps the best close viewpoint of Moel y Gaer iron-age hillfort. Although the lowest of the*

WALK 4

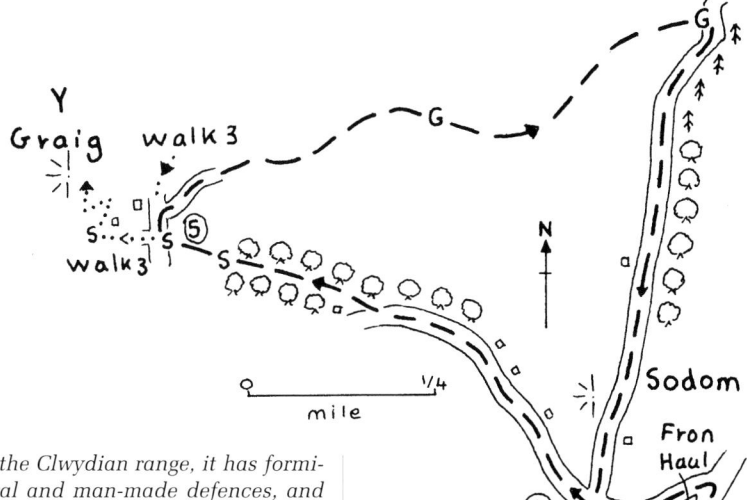

hillforts on the Clwydian range, it has formidable natural and man-made defences, and was able to defend the local population from invaders. Its entrance is at the northern end. The path continues half-LEFT down over two fields and on to an enclosed track leading to a lane met by point **3**. The path now follows the lane down past a wood, and two houses, taking a LEFT fork down to reach the main road at Bodfari. Turn RIGHT along the pavement, and at the Spar shop take the side road RIGHT (*Maes-y-Graig*) to soon rejoin your outward path back to the start, where you can enjoy a relaxing drink. *The Church of St. Stephen, with its large medieval tower and fine views from the churchyard, is well worth a visit.*

About the author, David Berry ...

David has lived and worked in this area of North Wales for over 25 years, and appreciates the beauty and history of its landscape, which he would like to share with others. A keen and experienced walker, he is equally at home taking a country ramble or walking to a mountain top. He has also undertaken many long distance walks, including coast to coast crossings of Wales, Scotland and England.

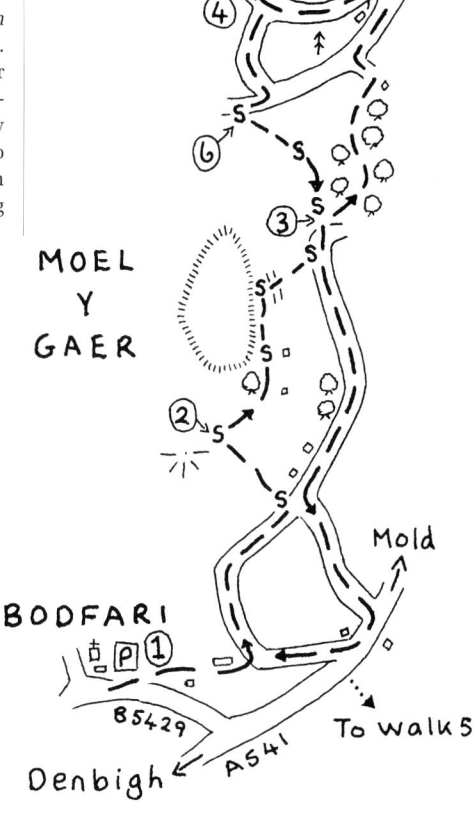

1 Follow the road opposite the telephone box, and then, opposite a lane, take a path on your left, crossing two fields to reach a road, where you turn RIGHT to pick up Offa's Dyke Path coming in from the left. *Nearby the former Mold – Denbigh branch railway line ran between 1869-1962. This is quite hard to believe, given the tranquillity of the setting!* At a T junction go RIGHT, then turn LEFT up a lane. *Ahead lie the bracken-covered slopes of Moel-y-Parc.* On reaching a post-box in a wall ahead, turn RIGHT to cross a stile by *Grove Goch. Note also the clock tower on nearby Grove Hall.*

2 Head half-LEFT to a stile in the field corner, and on with the fence on your left to the next stile. Now head half-LEFT up a slope to cross two fields. *Pause to look back across to Bodfari, with its church tower and the hill-fort of Moel-y-Gaer, rising above the rooftop of Grove Hall.* Continue in same direction, passing a marker post and carrying on to cross a stile by a gate. Turn RIGHT to follow the fence on your right to reach a waymarked path junction.

3 Here you turn sharp LEFT, leaving Offa's Dyke Path, to follow a wide green bridleway through a gate. Carry on along an enclosed and level green track. When the track splits, take the right hand fork up to a gate, and on through the edge of small wood to pass through another gate. A delightful green bridleway now takes you steadily up the side of a little known valley, then winds left and right to reach the shoulder of a hill. *At the head of the valley, pause to enjoy great views down to Bodfari, the distant coast and the mountains of Snowdonia. There are also good views looking south along the Clwydians from the shoulder.* Continue ahead to join a green track which descends south down a valley, overlooked by the conical hill of *Moel-y-Parc* with its TV transmitter mast, to pass *Fron Haul* and a ruined cottage.

4 The track soon swings left to rejoin Offa's Dyke Path and continues down to cross a stream. *The walk can be shortened by continuing ahead as the track swings left, to reach a green bridleway and on to point 7.* Continue along the track as it climbs gradual-

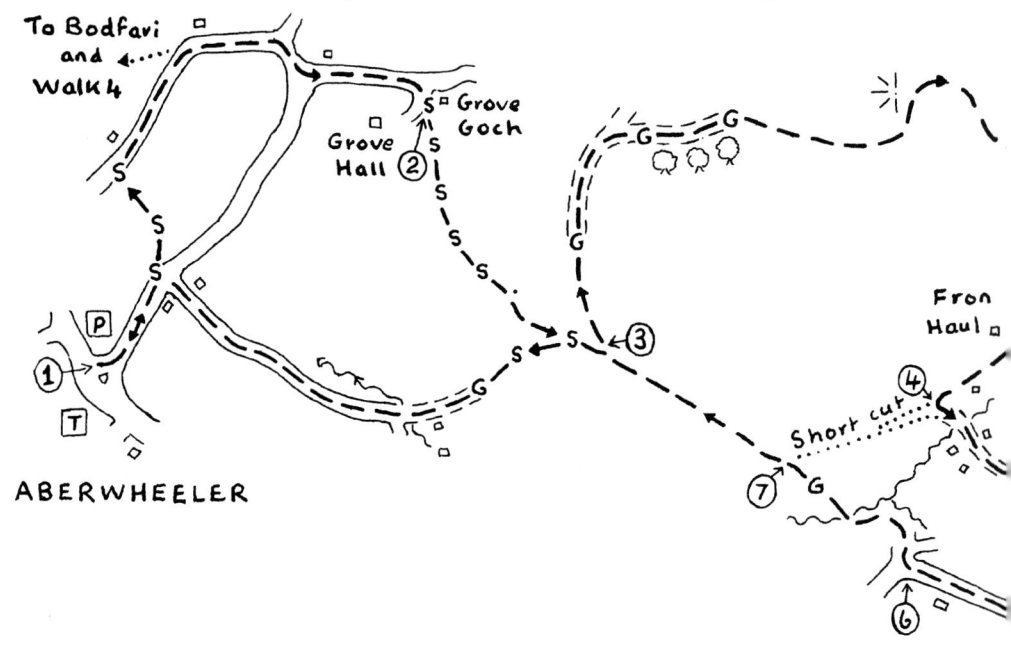

WALK 5

ly, passing old farm buildings and on into open country. Pass a derelict farm and continue through a gate, where the track levels out and meets others. Bear RIGHT to cross a stile beneath a clump of trees, and follow a track for 100 yards.

5 When the track bends left, leave Offa's Dyke Path, to follow the fence on your right down to a hidden gate. Ahead is a delightful wide green path, which gradually descends the hillside before swinging right to cross a stream, and continues on through a silver birch wood to reach a lane. *The upper part of this section is the remains of a Roman road, heading up from the Vale of Clwyd via Llandyrnog to pass over the hill*

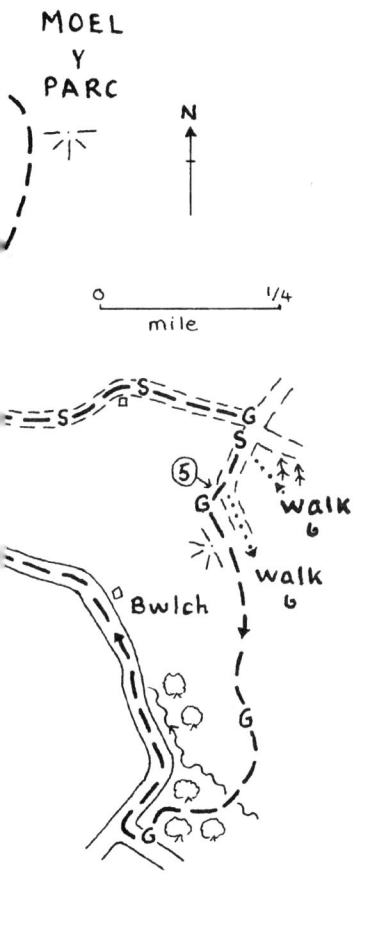

Walk 5

BENEATH MOEL-Y-PARC

DESCRIPTION This 5½-walk explores attractive and little known valleys, along with the lower slopes of Moel-y-Parc, using several superb green bridleways and even a short section of Roman road. It is good quality walking with panoramic views. This route can easily be shortened to 3¾ miles. Allow about 3 hours.

START Centre of Aberwheeler village. SJ 096694.

DIRECTIONS Take the A543/A541 from Denbigh towards Mold. Just before Bodfari turn right on the B5429 (Llanbedr/Llandyrnog) to reach Aberwheeler after ½ mile. Park in the lay-by, just beyond a play area, opposite *Bro Lleweni*.

and down to *Afonwen*, then on to *Caerwys*. It provides panoramic views of the Vale and beyond. Turn RIGHT and then RIGHT again at a T junction, to follow a quiet lane down into an attractive hidden valley, past *Bwlch Farm* and a cottage.

6 Where the lane bends left, turn RIGHT to go down an enclosed path, below the entrance to *Bwlch Isaf Farm*; soon following, and then crossing, a stream. Head uphill to reach a gate and then on up the slope to join a wide bridleway by a marker post.

7 Follow this delightful green way to the LEFT around the hillside to a fingerpost, and then go half-LEFT down to cross a stile. Now head straight down two fields, to pass through a gate by a house. Go down the access track, passing *Tyn-y-Celyn* and along a lane to reach a road, which you follow back to Aberwheeler.

Walk 6
PENYCLODDIAU

DESCRIPTION This 5-mile route follows Offa's Dyke Path, and rises to the large iron-age fort before returning along a high-level track contouring round the hill-side. It provides excellent walking and superb panoramic views. It is one of the author's favourite walks – in all seasons. Allow about 2½ hours.

START From the Llangwyfan Forestry car park. SJ 139668.

DIRECTIONS *From Denbigh*, take the road to Llandyrnog at the large roundabout on the southern end of the by-pass. After nearly 3 miles, at the next small roundabout, go ahead by 'The Kimnel Arms', and then at a cross-roads, turn left where signposted to Llangwyfan. After ½ mile, when you meet a right turn, continue ahead. Soon the road begins winding its way up a wooded side valley. After just over a mile you reach a forestry car park on the left, at the top of the pass. *From Mold*, take the A541 towards Denbigh, and then turn off left for Nannerch. As you enter the village, take the first road left, and continue for about 3 miles, towards Llandyrnog. The car park is on the right at the head of the valley.

1 Go through the small gate and continue straight ahead up the forestry track, to pick up the waymarked Offa's Dyke Path rising steadily alongside the edge of a forestry plantation. Cross a stile which gives access to the open hillside. *This point offers your first panoramic view looking down and across the Vale of Clwyd.* The path follows a series of marker posts to the summit of Penycloddiau. *Penycloddiau means 'The hill of the trenches'. The fort occupies a commanding heather and bilberry covered hilltop. It is the largest hill-fort on the Clwydians and one of the largest in Wales. Its interior is ½ mile long and it encloses an area of some 24 hectares, within a single substantial grass-covered rampart, strengthened at its northern end. There is evidence of level hut platforms within the fort. The views on a clear day are breathtaking. To the north, the Clwydians running from Moel-y-Parc north towards Prestatyn and Rhyl; to the north-west, the North Wales coast leading to The Great Orme; to the west, beyond the Vale of Clwyd to the distant mountains of Snowdonia; towards the south-west, the mountains of Arenig, Cadair Idris, and the Arans; to the south, Moel Arthur with its hill-fort and the distinctive ruined tower on the top of Moel Famau, and beyond to the Llantisilio Mountains and the distant Berwyn range; to the east, the distant Cheshire Plain; to the north-east, Halkyn Mountain, the Wirral, Liverpool, and beyond to the Pennines, the Lancashire coast and Blackpool.* The path leaves the summit to drop down to a stile and on across the broad grassy ridge to gradually descend to meet a track by a clump of trees.

2 You now leave Offa's Dyke Path to head LEFT with this delightful track as it contours round the flanks of Penycloddiau. *The track provides relaxed walking and the opportunity to enjoy in more detail the panoramic views covering the full extent of The Vale of Clwyd. To the west and south-west lie the medieval market towns of Denbigh and Ruthin respectively.* The route is clear and occasionally gated, passing a large old water tank, and areas of attractive mature woodland.

3 Shortly after the second wood, and just before a gate across the track, bear LEFT to go through a small wooden gate giving access to a plantation. A gently rising path will now take you through the forest back to the car park. *Note that by continuing on the track through the gate you can link with* **Walk 7** *at point* **2** *to make a combined circuit of 7¼ miles.*

WALK 6

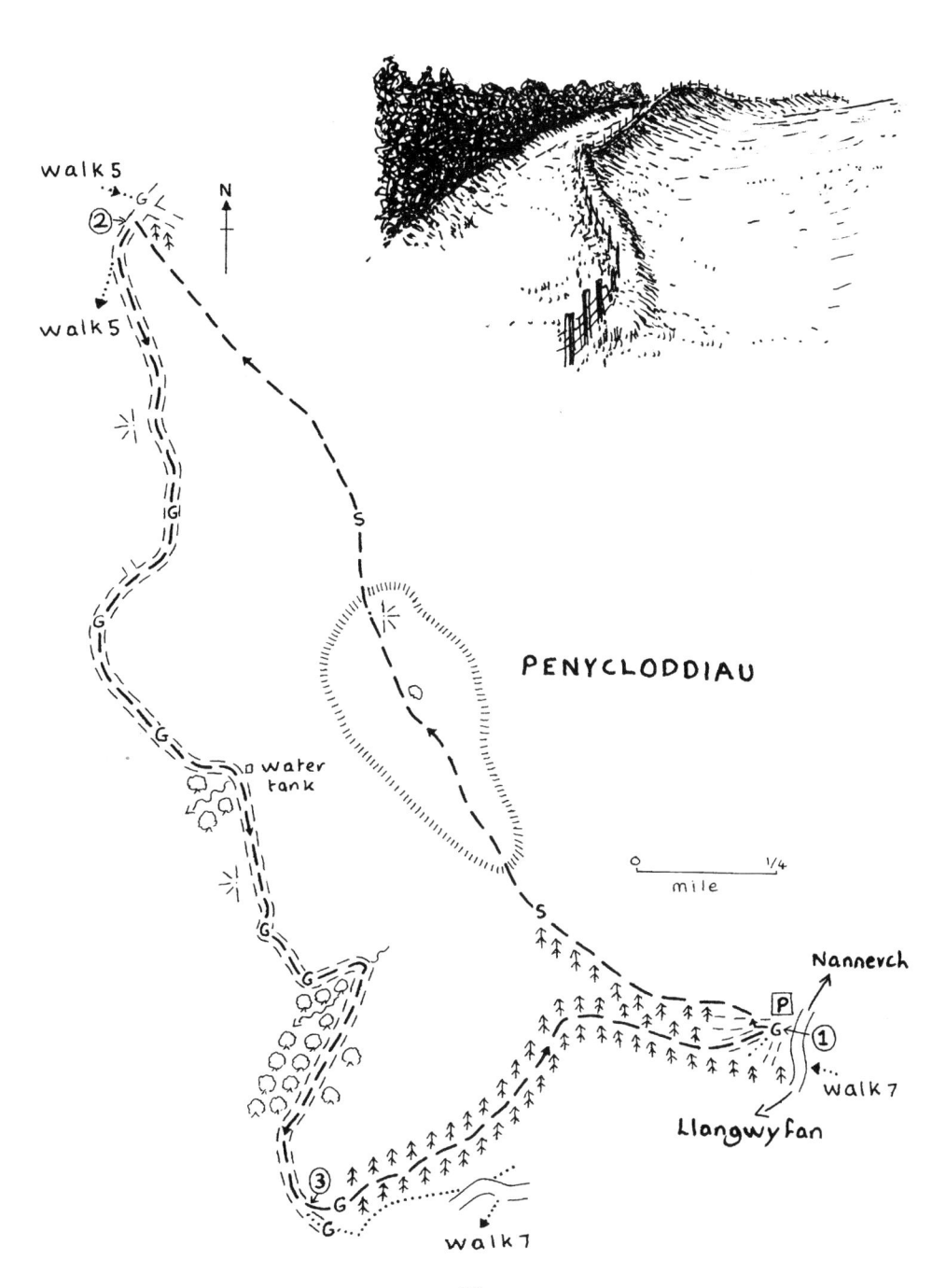

PENYCLODDIAU

walk 5
walk 5
water tank
Nannerch
walk 7
Llangwyfan
walk 7

Walk 7

MOEL ARTHUR

DESCRIPTION This 4-mile walk takes you on a good path through a forest, then on an attractive bridleway which winds its way up a little known valley to the top of a pass. Here it follows Offa's Dyke Path on a short, steady climb to visit the iron-age fort on the summit of Moel Arthur, where there are panoramic views. Allow about 2 hours.

START From the Llangwyfan Forestry car park. SJ 139668. An alternative start can be made from Moel Arthur car park at SJ 148658. See **Walk 8** for directions.

DIRECTIONS *From Denbigh*, take the road to Llandyrnog at the large roundabout on the southern end of the by-pass. After nearly 3 miles, at the next small roundabout, go ahead past 'The Kimnel Arms', and then, at a cross-roads, turn left where it is signposted to Llangwyfan. After ½-a-mile, when you meet a right turn, keep ahead, and soon the road begins winding its way up a wooded side-valley to reach a forestry car park on the left after just over a mile, at the top of the pass. *From Mold*, take the A541 towards Denbigh and then turn off left for Nannerch. As you enter the village, take the first road left for about 3 miles, towards Llandyrnog. The car park is on the right at the head of the valley.

1 Go through the small gate and then head half-LEFT to pick up a bridleway, between two forestry tracks, heading down through the trees. The bridleway crosses a forestry road, which it later joins and accompanies to a gate and a road, where you turn LEFT. After a few yards, turn RIGHT on a bridleway along an enclosed stony track to a gate, and then on past an unusually designed house. This delightful bridleway now contours round the hillside. *There are excellent views over the Vale of Clwyd and the distant mountains of Snowdonia.* The bridleway then turns to gently wind its way up the edge of an attractive wooded side-valley, and on along the open head of the valley to reach a road. *This last tree-lined section offers good views down the wooded valley to the Vale and the distant mountains. Look out for buzzards, which are seen in this area.*

3 Follow the quiet country road LEFT as it rises steadily above the edge of another side valley, overlooked by the bracken-covered flanks of Moel Llys-y-coed, to cross a cattle grid and reach a car parking area on the left. *Rising above you at 1494ft is the steep, conical, heather-covered hill of Moel Arthur, crowned by a circular iron-age hill-fort. It is a small, but prominent hillfort, defended on the naturally weaker northern side by two impressive ramparts and ditches. There is evidence of hut circles, and a hoard of Bronze Age copper axes have been found here.*

4 Take Offa's Dyke Path as it rises gently to cross over the lower right-hand shoulder of Moel Arthur to reach a marker post near a wooden gate. Here take a path LEFT to the top of Moel Arthur through the original fort entrance. *The sweeping views from here on a clear day are superb. To the north is Penycloddiau, with its mighty hill-fort, and Moel-y-Parc with its TV transmitter mast; to the north-west the North Wales coast sweeping towards the Great Orme; to the west, beyond the Vale of Clwyd the distant mountains of Snowdonia; towards the south-west, the mountains of Arenig, Cadair Idris, and The Arans; to the south, the distinctive ruined tower on the top of Moel Famau, and beyond to the Llantisilio Mountains and the distant Berwyn range; to the east, the distant Cheshire Plain and the distinctive shape of Beeston Castle hill; to the north-east, Halkyn Mountain, the Wirral, Liverpool, and beyond to the Pennines, the Lancashire coast and Blackpool.* Return to the main path which will take you down the grassy northern flanks of Moel Arthur to reach a road, where you turn RIGHT to return to the car park.

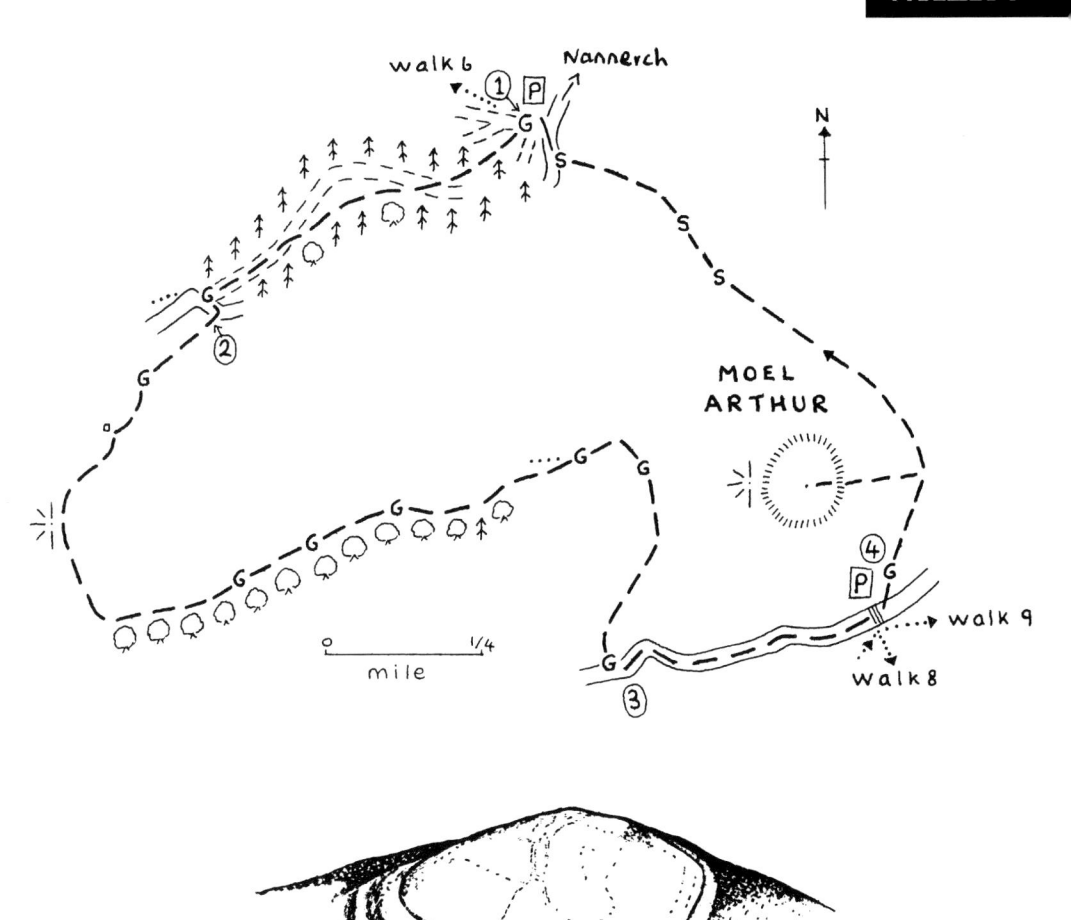

WALK 7

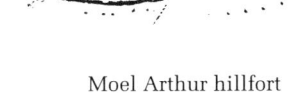

Moel Arthur hillfort

Looking west towards Snowdonia

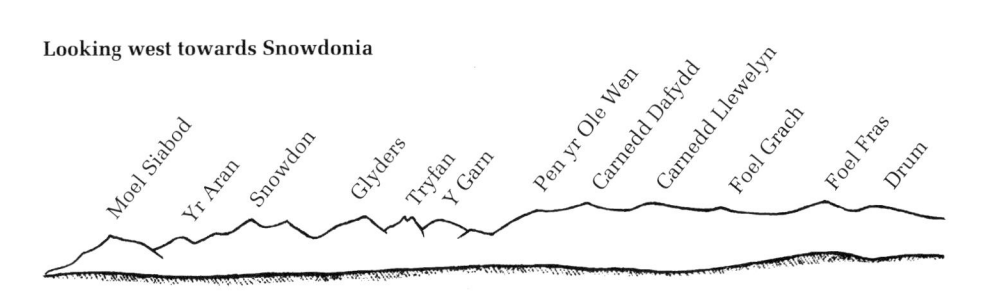

Moel Siabod, Yr Aran, Snowdon, Glyders, Tryfan, Y Garn, Pen yr Ole Wen, Carnedd Dafydd, Carnedd Llewelyn, Foel Grach, Foel Fras, Drum

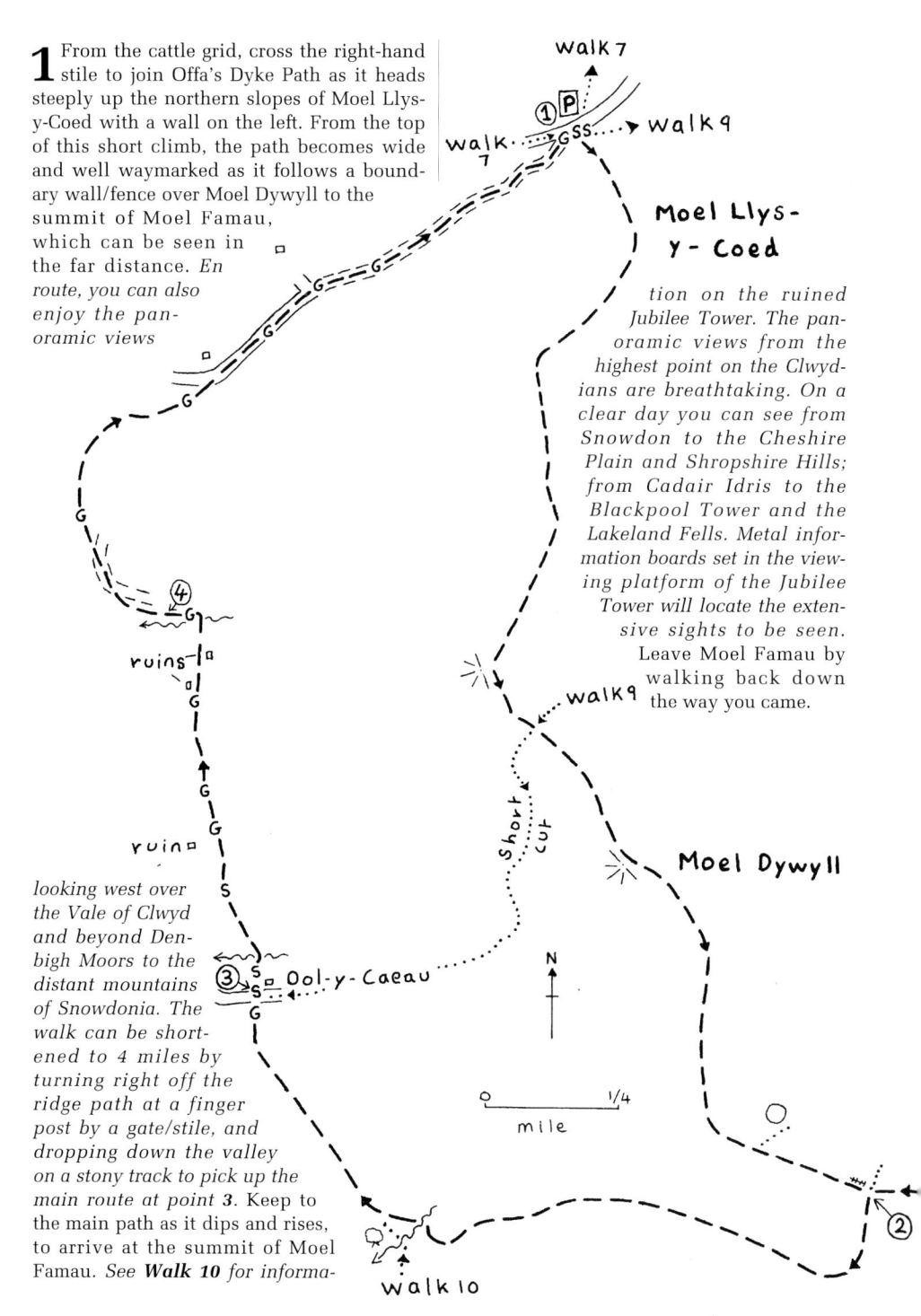

1 From the cattle grid, cross the right-hand stile to join Offa's Dyke Path as it heads steeply up the northern slopes of Moel Llys-y-Coed with a wall on the left. From the top of this short climb, the path becomes wide and well waymarked as it follows a boundary wall/fence over Moel Dywyll to the summit of Moel Famau, which can be seen in the far distance. *En route, you can also enjoy the panoramic views looking west over the Vale of Clwyd and beyond Denbigh Moors to the distant mountains of Snowdonia. The walk can be shortened to 4 miles by turning right off the ridge path at a finger post by a gate/stile, and dropping down the valley on a stony track to pick up the main route at point **3**. Keep to the main path as it dips and rises, to arrive at the summit of Moel Famau. See **Walk 10** for information on the ruined Jubilee Tower. The panoramic views from the highest point on the Clwydians are breathtaking. On a clear day you can see from Snowdon to the Cheshire Plain and Shropshire Hills; from Cadair Idris to the Blackpool Tower and the Lakeland Fells. Metal information boards set in the viewing platform of the Jubilee Tower will locate the extensive sights to be seen. Leave Moel Famau by walking back down the way you came.*

WALK 8

Walk 8

MOEL FAMAU AND THE WESTERN FRINGES

DESCRIPTION This exhilarating 6-mile walk explores part of the Moel Famau Country Park. It goes along the main northern ridge leading to Moel Famau, the highest of the Clwydian Hills, then back down an attractive side valley to return along the little known lower western flanks of the Clwydians. Apart from the initial short steep climb up Moel Llys-y-Coed, and the final climb up Moel Famau, which is optional, the walking is generally easily paced, offering superb panoramic views. An alternative 4-mile walk which leaves the ridge earlier is also an option. Allow about 3½ hours for the full route.
START At the car park beneath Moel Arthur.

SJ 148658.
DIRECTIONS *From Denbigh*, take the road to Llandyrnog at the large roundabout on the southern end of the by-pass. After nearly 3 miles, at the next small roundabout, go ahead past 'The Kimnel Arms', and then at a cross-roads, turn left signposted 'Llangwyfan'. After ½ mile, turn right, then take the first road left. This narrow road winds its way up a valley to a cattle grid and car park at the top of the pass. *Alternatively, travelling from Mold* towards Denbigh on the A541, take the next road left just after the turn-off to Cilcain, and follow the road up the valley to the car park.

2 At the foot of the steep slope, just before a short isolated section of wooden fencing, turn LEFT to follow a superb waymarked green route winding its way down the western slopes of an attractive side valley. *This is a permissive bridleway open to cyclists and horseriders, so take care.* At a finger-post, swing RIGHT to cross a stream and then LEFT to reach a marker post. Now head RIGHT with the bridleway, keeping the field boundary on the left, to reach a lane.

3 Cross the stile ahead by a cottage, and follow the path over a hidden stile in the field-corner and then on to cross a steam. Follow the field boundary on the left, over a stile, and then, as you approach a ruined cottage, head half-RIGHT up the field to go through a gate and on with the boundary on your right, to pass through another gate. The path continues ahead, soon through a gate, then past ruins, to cross a stream, before turning left through a gate (where it can be muddy!).

4 Follow the boundary on the left to briefly pick up a farm track. Where it heads half-right up the slope, keep straight ahead, close to the boundary on the left, to pass through a gate. Remain alongside the boundary, which soon swings right through a gate to reach a lane. Continue ahead with the lane, which soon becomes a rough farm track. Follow this track as it makes its way gently up the valley to the road and the start.

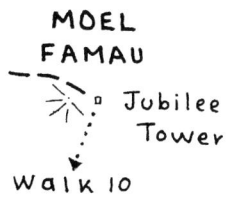

Walk 9

MOEL LLYS-Y-COED, CILCAIN AND CWM GAIN

DESCRIPTION A stimulating 5¼-mile walk exploring a valley and the foothills of Moel Famau, and visiting the attractive hillside village of Cilcain, with its ancient church and inn. Good paths and quiet country lanes make for enjoyable walking, with excellent views to be gained. The walk can be shortened by using a linked track/lane. Allow about 3 hours for the full route.
START Car park beneath Moel Arthur. SJ 148658. An alternative start can be made from the reservoir ⅓ mile south-west of Cilcain. SJ 172648.
DIRECTIONS See **Walk 8** for directions to Moel Arthur car park. To reach the alternative start, turn off the A541 Mold – Denbigh road for Cilcain, and turn right in the village centre, passing the White Horse Inn, then left by the church. Follow this minor road down to park near a small reservoir.

1 From the car park, go over the left of two stiles by the cattle grid. Head half-LEFT on a clear path which soon begins to climb steadily across the slopes of Moel Llys-y-Coed. *From the top of the rise there are good views towards Moel Arthur and the more northern hills of Penycloddiau and Moel y Parc, with the coast in the distance. To the north, beyond Halkyn Mount-ain, lie the Dee Estuary, Merseyside, and distant Lancashire. Further to the east, across the Cheshire Plain are the distinctive shapes of Beeston and Peckforton Hills.*

WALK 9

2 Go over a stile, and keep the field boundary on your right to cross a stile in the fence ahead. Head slightly RIGHT to pass through a gate and follow a path down alongside an old stone wall on your right to reach another stile. *To the south are lovely views over to the bracken-covered slopes of Moel Famau with its ruined Jubilee Tower.* The path continues ahead, now with the field boundary on your left, and on down to reach a quiet country lane. Follow the lane RIGHT, over a cross-roads *(where turning right can provide an alternative shorter route)* to eventually drop down into Cilcain.

3 *Cilcain is a small hillside settlement lying beneath the eastern slopes of Moel Famau. It was listed in the Doomsday Book of 1086, and is a meeting point of old drovers roads. A visit to St. Mary's Church is highly recommended. The earliest features of the double-naved building date from the 14th and 15thC. It contains a magnificent medieval oak roof with winged angels and splendid carvings, which is believed to have been brought to the church from another building – possibly Basingwerk Abbey – during the Dissolution of the Monasteries by Henry VIII in the early 16thC. The church contains other notable features which are detailed in a pamphlet available for visitors. The White Horse, a 16thC coaching inn is the last of seven inns that once existed in the area.* Leave the village by a road on the west side of the church to reach a small reservoir *(this is also an alternative start).*

4 Take the stony track off the bend in the road, on a bridleway leading up *Cwm Gain.* Pass two small reservoirs, and, when the track splits, keep ahead with the stream on your right. At a gate across the track, the bridleway bears half-LEFT through a small gate and then rises beside a large reservoir, soon swinging half-LEFT to cross a stream by two trees *making a very pleasant spot for a rest.* Continue ahead alongside an old stone wall on your right. This delightful bridleway rises steadily up the side of the valley to reach a stony track, which you follow LEFT to a gate/stile. Here it meets Offa's Dyke Path, which runs along the ridge.

5 Turning left will take you to the summit of Moel Famau on **Walk 8**. For those starting near Cilcain, the walk can be shortened, after enjoying the views, by following the track back down the valley to meet the road leading to the village. The main route crosses the stile and goes RIGHT up the slope on Offa's Dyke Path and along the open heather-clad ridge, before taking a short steep descent to the road beneath Moel Arthur, and the start. *This section offers panoramic views from the Vale of Clwyd to the coast; the mountains of Snowdonia and south down to Cadair Idris and the Arans. The final descent also provides an excellent viewpoint of Moel Arthur, with its iron-age fort.*

Walk 10

MOEL-Y-GAER AND MOEL FAMAU

DESCRIPTION This 5-mile route provides a fascinating exploration of the little known western flanks of the Clwydians, culminating in a long steady climb up to the top of Moel Famau – at 1820ft – the highest hill in the range. En route there is the opportunity to visit one of the most remote of the Clwydian hillforts. Paths are generally good and the panoramic views are excellent. Allow about 3½ hours.
START Car park at Bwlch Penbarras. SJ 162606.

DIRECTIONS From Mold take the A494 towards Ruthin. Shortly after passing Loggerheads Country Park, take a minor road right signposted 'Moel Famau Country Park'. Follow this road for 2 miles, passing the main car park, where there are toilets, until you reach a car park on the right, just beyond a cattle grid at the top of the pass. Alternative car parking is also available nearby.

1 Head north from the car park on the wide stony Offa's Dyke Path, which you soon leave at a waymark post, on a path angling left, to cross a stile and continue to a marker post. Here go half-RIGHT over rough ground down to a ladder stile. *There are impressive views ahead of the heather and bracken covered side ridges of the western Clwydians, stretching out like extended fingers. Standing a little aloof is the green topped hill of Moel-y-Gaer, with its distinctive ramparts. Moel-y-Gaer is a classic contour fort with a double circuit of ramparts, strengthened on its northern side by a third rampart. It is the only local hill-fort with a dog-leg entrance on the eastern side – this was a means of defending against an enemy's attack on the gates. It remains un-excavated, but there is possible evidence of 'hut platforms'.*

2 Head LEFT on a vague green track for 100 yards and, as it swings left, continue down over open pasture aiming for the right flank of the small gorse-capped hill ahead. Pick up a faint green track which takes you down the valley to a pair of gates. Pass through the RIGHT hand gate and follow the fence on your left down to a gate. Here, swing sharp RIGHT on a green track leading to a delightful side valley. After about 200 yards angle LEFT down to cross the stream and then rise with a path which soon swings left to reach a fence corner.

3 *For those wishing to visit the summit of Moel-y-Gaer, head north-east up the steep southern flanks of the hill. After admiring the supreme defensive position and remains of the hillfort, descend north-west down the northern slopes to pick up the main route at point 4.* The main route follows the field boundary on your left along the lower slopes of Moel-y-Gaer, until you meet a metal gate in this boundary. Go through the gate and then continue in the same direction following the line of a tree boundary on your left. The path soon swings slightly right to a gate.

4 Ignore the green track rising up the slope, but continue ahead to swing RIGHT to pass round to the right of a large area of gorse, crossing a stile and following the fence LEFT to cross a stream by a gate. The path now leads left, rising gently above and away from the stream to swing right by a clump of trees and a cottage. Follow the field boundary on your left, contouring the lower slopes. *There are fine views of the Vale of Clwyd and beyond.*

5 Shortly after passing a stream, turn sharp RIGHT on a delightful waymarked green bridleway, which crosses a stream and rises steadily up the flanks of an attractive side valley to reach a small plateau and Offa's Dyke Path, running along the main ridge of

20

WALK 10

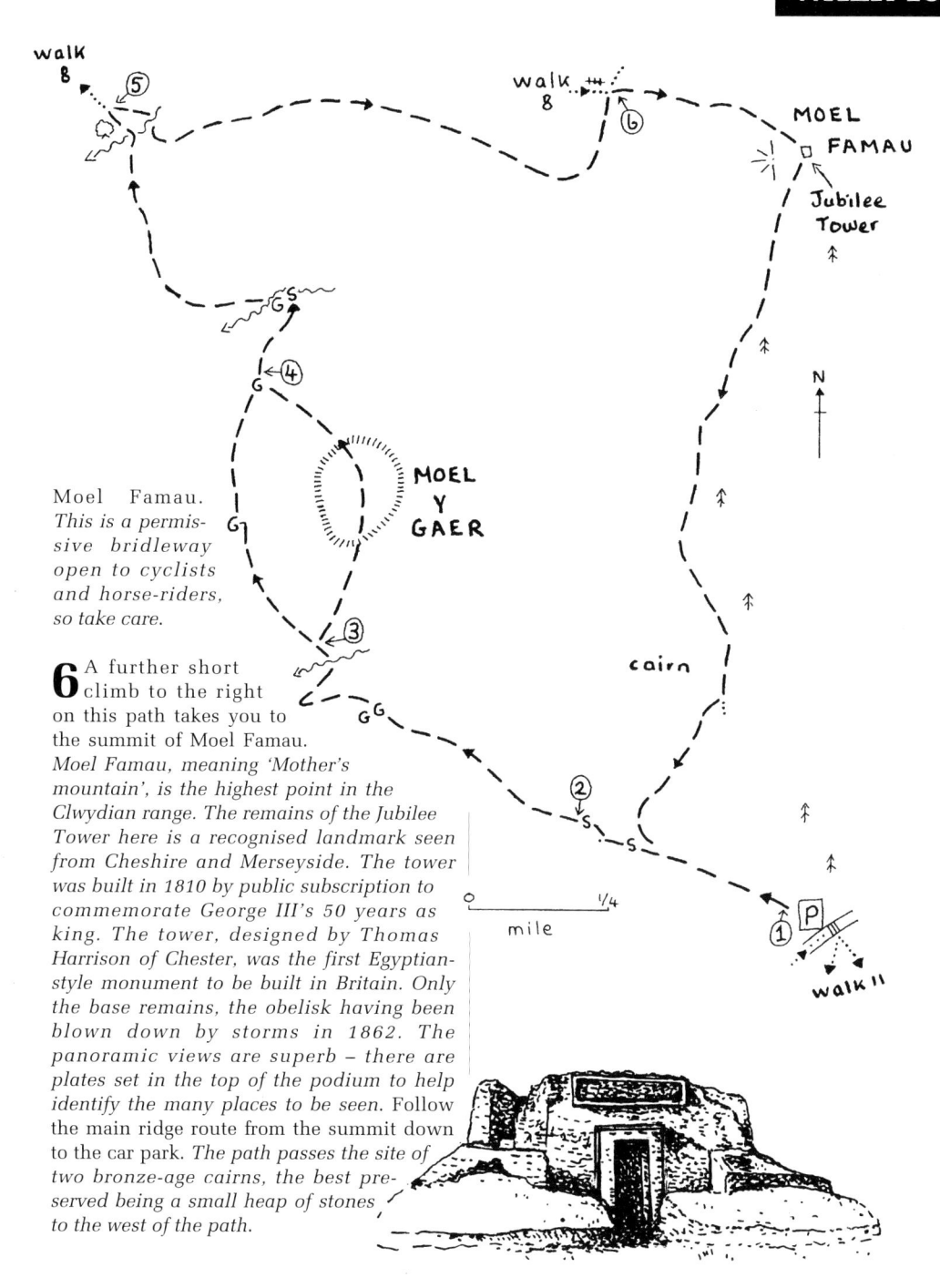

Moel Famau. This is a permissive bridleway open to cyclists and horse-riders, so take care.

6 A further short climb to the right on this path takes you to the summit of Moel Famau. *Moel Famau, meaning 'Mother's mountain', is the highest point in the Clwydian range. The remains of the Jubilee Tower here is a recognised landmark seen from Cheshire and Merseyside. The tower was built in 1810 by public subscription to commemorate George III's 50 years as king. The tower, designed by Thomas Harrison of Chester, was the first Egyptian-style monument to be built in Britain. Only the base remains, the obelisk having been blown down by storms in 1862. The panoramic views are superb – there are plates set in the top of the podium to help identify the many places to be seen. Follow the main ridge route from the summit down to the car park. The path passes the site of two bronze-age cairns, the best preserved being a small heap of stones to the west of the path.*

Walk 11

MOEL FENLLI AND CWM BLAENNANT

DESCRIPTION This interesting 6-mile walk visits an impressive iron-age hill-fort before meandering in open country along Offa's Dyke Path to Clwyd Gate. The return route takes you to the little known western fringes of the Clwydians, through attractive woodland, and explores a delightful hidden valley beneath Moel Fenlli. Apart from the initial short steep climb up Moel Fenlli, which can be eased by taking an alternative path that avoids the summit, the route offers good steady walking on clear paths, with excellent views throughout. Allow about 3½ hours.

START Car park at Bwlch Penbarras. SJ 162606.

DIRECTIONS From Mold take the A494 towards Ruthin. Shortly after passing Loggerheads Country Park, take a minor road right signposted 'Moel Famau Country Park'. Follow this road for 2 miles, passing a car park with toilets, to reach a car park on the right, just beyond a cattle grid at the top of the pass.

1 From the gate by the cattle grid there is a choice of routes. The main route follows a path signposted to Moel Fenlli, on through a gate by a small pond to pick up a waymarked path at the edge of a forest. The path zig-zags its way up the northern slopes of the hill, crossing the mighty ramparts of this iron-age fort, to reach the summit. Alternatively, you can follow the less demanding, but delightful, Offa's Dyke Path which climbs steadily along the facing hillside to contour round the lower ramparts of Moel Fenlli to point **2**. *Moel Fenlli is an impressive hillfort with double ramparts defending the north and east of the hill, with its main entrance on the west side. The fort had a good supply of water from its own spring and from ones nearby. The distant views on a clear day are breathtaking. To the south, Llandegla Moors, the Llantisilio and Berwyn Mountains; to the south-west the Arans, Cadair Idris and Arenig; to the west, the mountains of Snowdonia; to the north, Moel Famau and beyond to the coast sweeping westwards towards the Great Orme; to the north-east, Halkyn Mountain, Merseyside, and distant Lancashire; to the east, the Cheshire Plain.* Head south from the summit cairn to pick up a stony path running right with a rampart. Follow this down to join the Offa's Dyke Path at a marker post, where you turn LEFT.

2 Keep with the path as it skirts the southern flanks of the hill, before dropping sharply down to pass the end of a conifer plantation to reach a field. The path heads half-LEFT to follow a fence to a stile and on past a wood to the field corner. Here you turn RIGHT and follow the waymarked path through two fields, a short section of woodland, and then a narrow field to reach a farm track, which takes you to the Mold-Ruthin road. *To the east can be seen an area of limestone, once extensively mined for lead.* Follow the road to the RIGHT to the entrance of the Clwyd Gate Inn, where you can stop for a drink. TAKE CARE – THIS IS A BUSY ROAD! Cross the road, turn RIGHT and then go half-LEFT down a lane.

3 After a few yards, you leave Offa's Dyke Path by crossing a stile on your right. Follow the field boundary down to cross another stile and on down the edge of a small wood. At a track take the LEFT fork, and soon go RIGHT over a stile, by-passing a cottage, and continuing on through delightful woodland to enter a field. Now head half-RIGHT to cross a stile, and continue half-RIGHT to pass the left hand side of a small pond half-way down the next field. *This is a good place for a picnic.*

WALK 11

4 Ignore a stile ahead, but turn RIGHT alongside the pond and on over a stile to follow a wide green path up through the edge of an attractive wood. You reach a track which you follow to the LEFT, soon to rejoin the Mold-Ruthin road. Turn LEFT and walk WITH CARE along the grass verge for about 100 yards to cross the road to a footpath sign.

5 Follow a stony track along the edge of a wood and stay with it as it swings right to pass above Cae-Mawr Farm. The way ahead is on a delightful old green track leading towards the head of an attractive side valley. Cwm Blaennant is a haven for wildlife and you should keep your eyes open for buzzards, kestrels and other hawks.

6 After passing through a gate, continue on a narrow path alongside a ruined stone wall, staying with it as it turns left. *Towering above you are the heather and bracken-covered slopes of Moel Fenlli. It is difficult to imagine that your outward path is just above you!.* Just after the wall peters out, cross a fence ahead, and turn LEFT, walking down with a partly hidden stream and keeping the field boundary on the left, to pass a small wood. You reach a stony track, which will take you to a road. Follow this quiet old drovers road RIGHT, winding up the edge of attractive Cwm Ceunant. *Enjoy the tremendous views on your way back to the start.*

Walk 12

MOEL LLANFAIR AND COED PLAS-Y-NANT

DESCRIPTION An interesting 6-mile walk combining the delights of an open high-level path with tremendous views, and the opportunity to explore two little-known side-valleys. Starting from one of the main passes through the Clwydians, the route rises with Offa's Dyke Path to skirt the flanks of Moel Gyw and Moel Llanfair. It then heads down on a track and quiet lane to briefly flirt with the green fields of the Vale of Clwyd before following a bridleway up through the attractive woodland of Coed Plas-y-Nant to the top of the pass. An enjoyable 4-mile alternative walk involves completing a circuit of Moel Llanfair, then returns on your outward route. Allow about 3 hours, or 2 hours for the alternative route.
START Clwyd Gate Inn. SJ 164582.
DIRECTIONS From Ruthin follow the A494 towards Mold for about 3 miles, to reach the Clwyd Gate Inn at the top of the pass. Parking is allowed in the car park, but the landlord would appreciate being informed. Outside opening hours, please notify the Motel reception.

1 Leave the car park and cross the road WITH CARE, to turn RIGHT and then half-LEFT down a lane, which soon becomes a stony track. Offa's Dyke Path follows this track, passing houses and a farm entrance, before crossing a waymarked stile to bear left up a field to another stile. Continue ahead over two grassy hillocks to cross another stile. Follow a green track as it contours around Moel Gyw. *This superb green track offers panoramic views of the Vale of Clwyd, from the coast to the Llantisilio Mountains.*

2 At a waymark post, the path heads half-right to reach a stony track. *Just beyond the post at the top of the green track lies the 'Garreg Lwyd' (grey stone), marking an ancient route over the hills between Ruthin and Llanarmon.* Follow the stony track as it winds gently right down the valley. Just before a gate across the track, turn LEFT over a stile to follow the path with the fence on your right as it contours around Moel Llanfair to reach a stony track. *Here you can shorten the walk by following a path that goes round the eastern slopes of Moel Llanfair to rejoin the outward green track below the 'Garreg Lwyd'.*

3 Follow this track down to the RIGHT, soon swinging RIGHT to drop gently into a wide valley reaching a farm, with an interesting barn conversion, and a lane. Continue down the lane, passing Sinet (*note the dovecot and 'farming' weather-vane*), and on with the leafy lane to a T-junction. Take the road RIGHT to reach another main junction, where you turn RIGHT towards Llanbedr. Follow this road for ½ a mile, passing a cattle breeding centre.

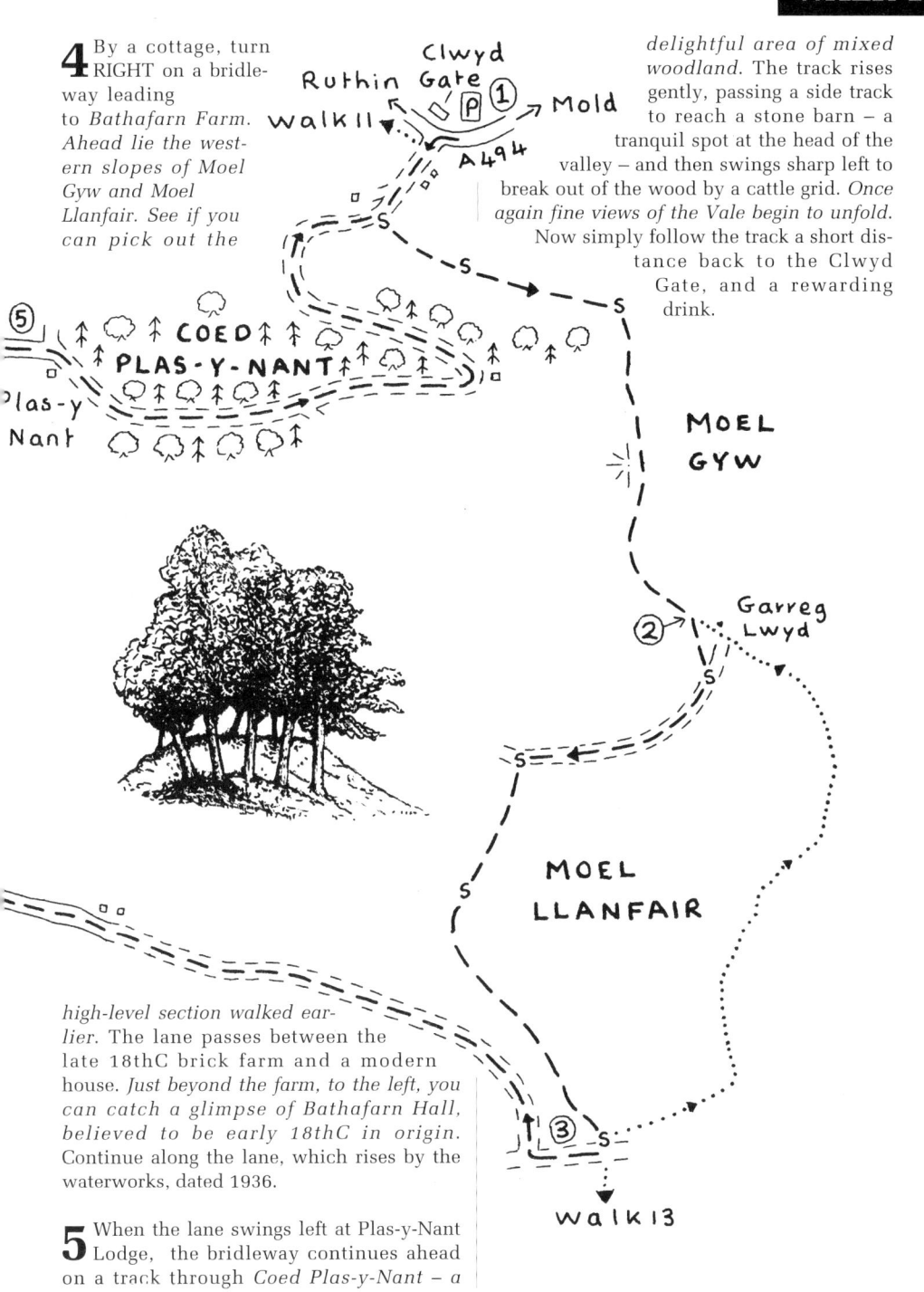

WALK 12

4 By a cottage, turn RIGHT on a bridleway leading to *Bathafarn Farm*. Ahead lie the western slopes of Moel Gyw and Moel Llanfair. See if you can pick out the high-level section walked earlier. The lane passes between the late 18thC brick farm and a modern house. *Just beyond the farm, to the left, you can catch a glimpse of Bathafarn Hall, believed to be early 18thC in origin.* Continue along the lane, which rises by the waterworks, dated 1936.

5 When the lane swings left at Plas-y-Nant Lodge, the bridleway continues ahead on a track through *Coed Plas-y-Nant* – a delightful area of mixed woodland. The track rises gently, passing a side track to reach a stone barn – a tranquil spot at the head of the valley – and then swings sharp left to break out of the wood by a cattle grid. *Once again fine views of the Vale begin to unfold.* Now simply follow the track a short distance back to the Clwyd Gate, and a rewarding drink.

Walk 13

MOEL Y PLAS

DESCRIPTION This 5-mile walk explores the attractive western edges of the Clwydians near Graigfechan, and includes a splendid short section of Offa's Dyke Path over Moel y Plas, offering panoramic views. A mixture of woodland, limestone, pastureland, a small lake, scenic side valleys and open fells, all on on good paths, tracks and quiet lanes, make this an interesting and enjoyable route, with the bonus of a fine old inn at the finish. A slightly shorter alternative return route is identified. Allow about 3 hours.

START The Three Pigeons Inn, Graigfechan. SJ 147544.

DIRECTIONS From Ruthin, take the A494 towards Mold. After about 1 mile turn right along the B5429 for 3 miles to reach The Three Pigeons Inn, in Graigfechan. Parking is allowed in the car park, *but the landlord would appreciate being informed.*

1 Walk south down the road, then turn LEFT on a waymarked bridleway. After 20 yards, at another waymark post, turn LEFT again to follow the bridleway up to a wide track. Follow it LEFT to pass a house and continue ahead through the trees, soon passing another house and a disused limekiln. *A feature of this locality is exposed limestone, small quarries and limekilns, which produced lime, particularly for use as a fertiliser.* Keep on through woodland, with a fence on your left.

2 Just before reaching a field, head half-RIGHT up past a holly tree, to follow a path just inside the wood boundary, to eventually emerge into the bottom of the field. Go ahead down an enclosed track and just before a gate by a building, cross a stile up on your right, and then bear LEFT to another stile and a road. Follow the road LEFT between cottages, passing a side road. *Note a Victorian letter-box set in the wall of Plas Tirion.*

3 Just before a road junction, go through a gate on your right, and then on through another. Follow the field boundary to cross a stile ahead by a recently created small lake. *This is a haven for wildlife, and worth a short stop to watch the coots and other waterfowl.* A path takes you right over a footbridge, through a small copse and into a field. Head half-LEFT to cross a stile onto the gravel drive of the house ahead. Go ahead, and, just as the drive swings left, look for a marker post in the bushes. The path leaves the garden by a stile, and goes on to a gate at the entrance to *Sinet Farm*, to reach a lane.

4 Follow the quiet lane to the RIGHT. Just beyond an interesting barn conversion, it becomes a track which winds its way steadily up a wide valley to reach the top of the pass, crossed by Offa's Dyke Path. Cross the stile on the right and follow the well waymarked path up over the flanks of Moel-y-Plas and down past a transmitter mast to reach a minor road. *As you descend Moel-y-Plas, there are excellent views down to Llyn Gweryd and beyond to Llandegla Moors, and over the southern end of the Clwydian range towards the Llantisilio Mountains. The walk can be shortened by swinging right on a path down an attractive side valley before you reach the mast.*

5 You now leave Offa's Dyke Path by turning RIGHT over a stile opposite the drive to *Pen-y-Ffrith Fly Fishery*. Follow a pleasant track through two gates, down and along the edge of an attractive side valley. When the track splits, take the right fork to reach a lane by *Pen-y-Bryn* farm. Follow the lane down, and just beyond *Din Bidryn*, cross a stile on the right. The path now follows the boundary on the right, before bearing down half-LEFT to cross a stile in the field corner. Continue half-LEFT, over a stile and through the garden of a house, to reach a road. Turn LEFT and follow the road past houses to a T junction. Turn RIGHT to return to the start and a relaxing drink in The Three Pigeons Inn.

WALK 13

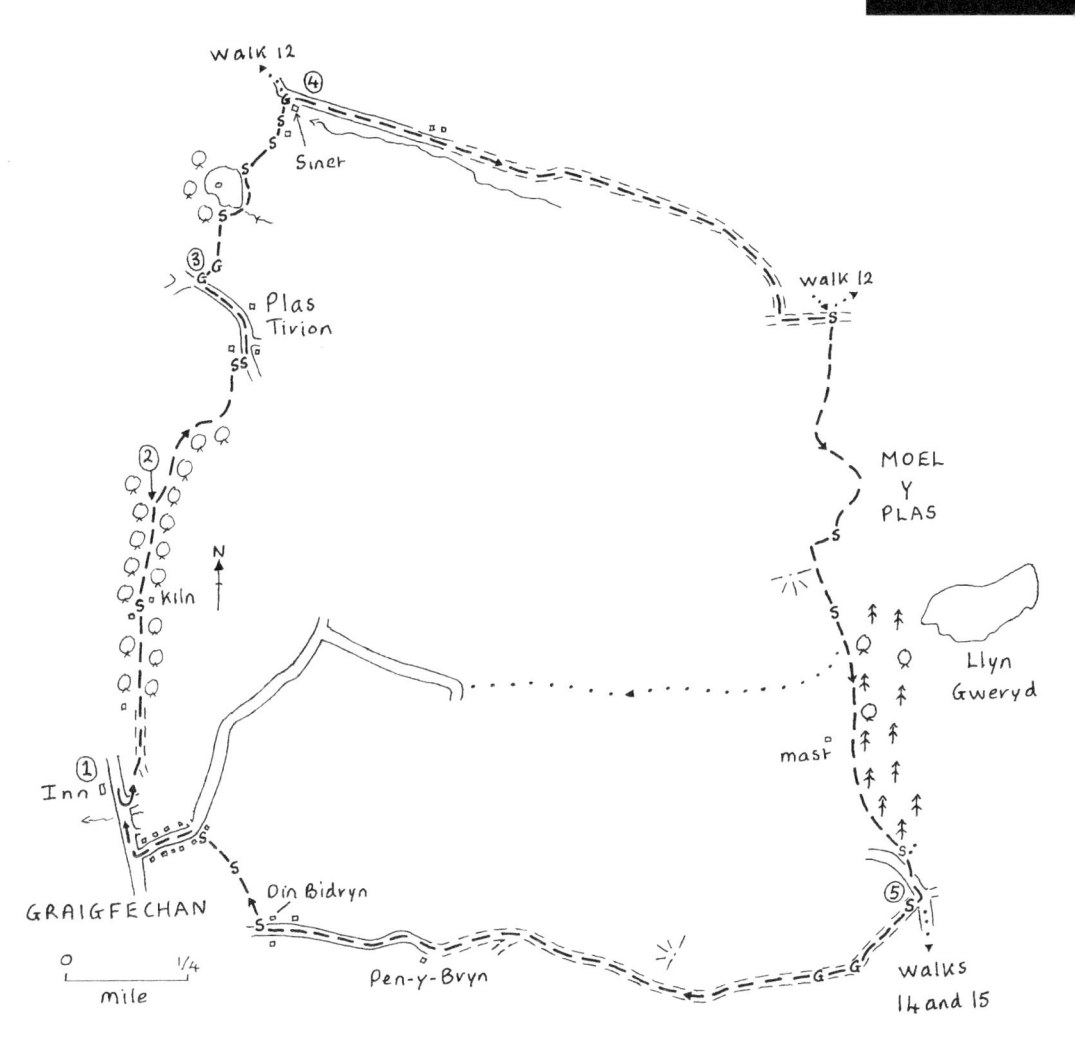

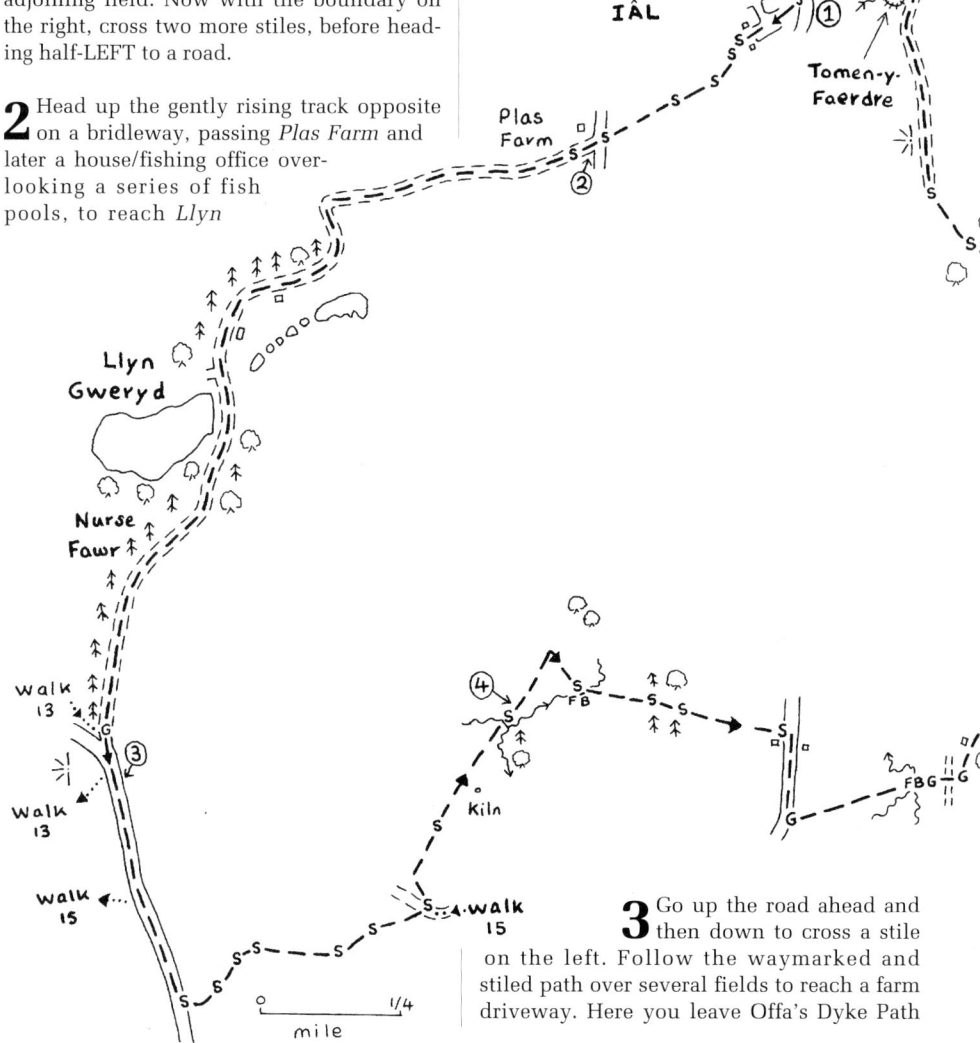

*B*efore starting the walk, a visit to the Church of St. Garmon is highly recommended. This fascinating medieval double-naved church, extensively restored during the 1730s, has many outstanding features, one of the finest being a brass chandelier made in Bruges in about 1500. A guide pamphlet is available.

1 From the church, take a path opposite, signposted to *Nurse Fawr*. The path passes through a small housing estate to enter a field. After a few yards, cross a stile into the adjoining field. Now with the boundary on the right, cross two more stiles, before heading half-LEFT to a road.

2 Head up the gently rising track opposite on a bridleway, passing *Plas Farm* and later a house/fishing office overlooking a series of fish pools, to reach *Llyn Gweryd*. This became a reservoir about 1870, and is now a popular fishing lake. Take a track LEFT by the end of the lake and through an area of young mixed woodland to pass through a gate to join Offa's Dyke Path and a road. *There are lovely views looking west down towards the Vale of Clwyd.* You can link in with **Walks 13** *(point 5)* here, and shortly **Walk 15** *(point 3)*.

3 Go up the road ahead and then down to cross a stile on the left. Follow the waymarked and stiled path over several fields to reach a farm driveway. Here you leave Offa's Dyke Path

28

WALK 14

Walk 14

LLYN GWERYD AND LIMESTONE PASTURES

DESCRIPTION An easy 4¾-mile walk that introduces you to the mixed scenic delights of an area around Llanarmon-yn-ial. It visits the gentle green eastern flanks of the Clwydians, takes in a hillside lake, and explores a rich wooded limestone area. Other highlights include a medieval church, an 11thC fortress, and an ancient cave. Allow about 3 hours.
START St. Garmon Church, Llanarmon-yn-ial. SJ 191561.
DIRECTIONS From the A494 Ruthin-Mold road, take the B5430 towards Llanarmon-yn-ial, and after 2 miles turn right on the B5431 to enter the village. Go past the 18thC Raven Inn and, as the main road swings left, continue straight ahead, passing the post office. Park on the roadside in *Maes Ial*.

by crossing the stile opposite. Bear sharp LEFT to go through a field gap, and then go half-RIGHT, first to a stile and then on above a limekiln, down to cross a stile by a stream and a wood. *Lime-kilns are a feature of this area, and the lime produced was used by local farmers as a fertiliser.*

4 Now head over a large field towards a small wood, and when half-way across, turn RIGHT to cross a stile and footbridge over the stream. The path now rises half-LEFT to pass straight through a small wood to a large field. Head slightly RIGHT to the field corner and a road, which you follow RIGHT. Soon turn LEFT on a bridleway, which is at first enclosed, to cross a field and footbridge. Go through a gate and across a farm track to pass through a small gate. The bridleway skirts a farm, and goes on through a gate to rise gently with a field boundary. *The nature of the land begins to change with the appearance of exposed limestone.*

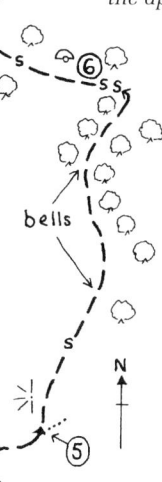

5 At a metal gate on your right, leave the bridleway and head half-LEFT up the limestone-decked slope to cross a stile in a wall corner. You now unexpectedly find yourself on a golfing green. *The next section passes through a small golf course set amongst delightful tree-covered but exposed limestone ridges.* Keep to the field boundary on the left, passing a warning bell used to alert golfers, and on to another golf tee/bell, and then down to swing LEFT by no. 5 tee, to cross two stiles in the field corner.

6 Ignore a stile on your right, but go ahead alongside a caravan park boundary to soon drop down to cross a ladder-stile. Keep ahead, through an old wall-gap, over another large ladder-stile and on to enter and follow an old green lane. *This was once an important road used to convey people by carriage to Llanarmon Church. The diverse geological nature of this area can now be seen: the rolling green hills of the Clwydians, composed of Silurian shales, and*

the limestone crags ahead, more reminiscent parts of the Yorkshire Dales. Suddenly, Llanarmon comes into view and further surprises await you. On your left, as you near a road, you will see the remains of Tomen-y-Faerdre – a medieval fortress, possibly 11thC in origin. The mound or 'motte' forms part of a natural rock outcrop overlooking the River Alun, defended on the other sides by an artificial ditch. It originally supported a stone tower or 'bailey'. Opposite is a large cave where prehistoric remains have been found. At the road turn LEFT back to the start.

Before starting the walk, visit the church, which was entirely rebuilt in 1866. Interesting items include a medieval brass chandelier, an old font, and a Georgian window, which was made in 1800 for St. Asaph Cathedral.

1 Take the waymarked Offa's Dyke Path down a track between the church and the old rectory and on across a large field, following the course of the river Alun. The path then crosses a footbridge over the river, and follows the field boundary on the right to cross a partly hidden stile at the top of a rise. It continues ahead beside a small wood, over a footbridge and on to briefly accompany the river.

2 When the river swings right, continue ahead to cross a stile beside a gate, then go LEFT for a few yards, before turning RIGHT to accompany the boundary to the end of the field. Turn LEFT on an enclosed path to a road. *Lying to the east of this road are several caves, occupied by early man.* Go up the track opposite towards Chweleiriog Llwyd. *In a field on the left is St. Garmon's Well, once known for its healing properties.* Approaching the farm, the path heads left off the track over several fields to reach a road. Go RIGHT up the road and soon you reach a waymarked stile on your left, where you leave Offa's Dyke Path.

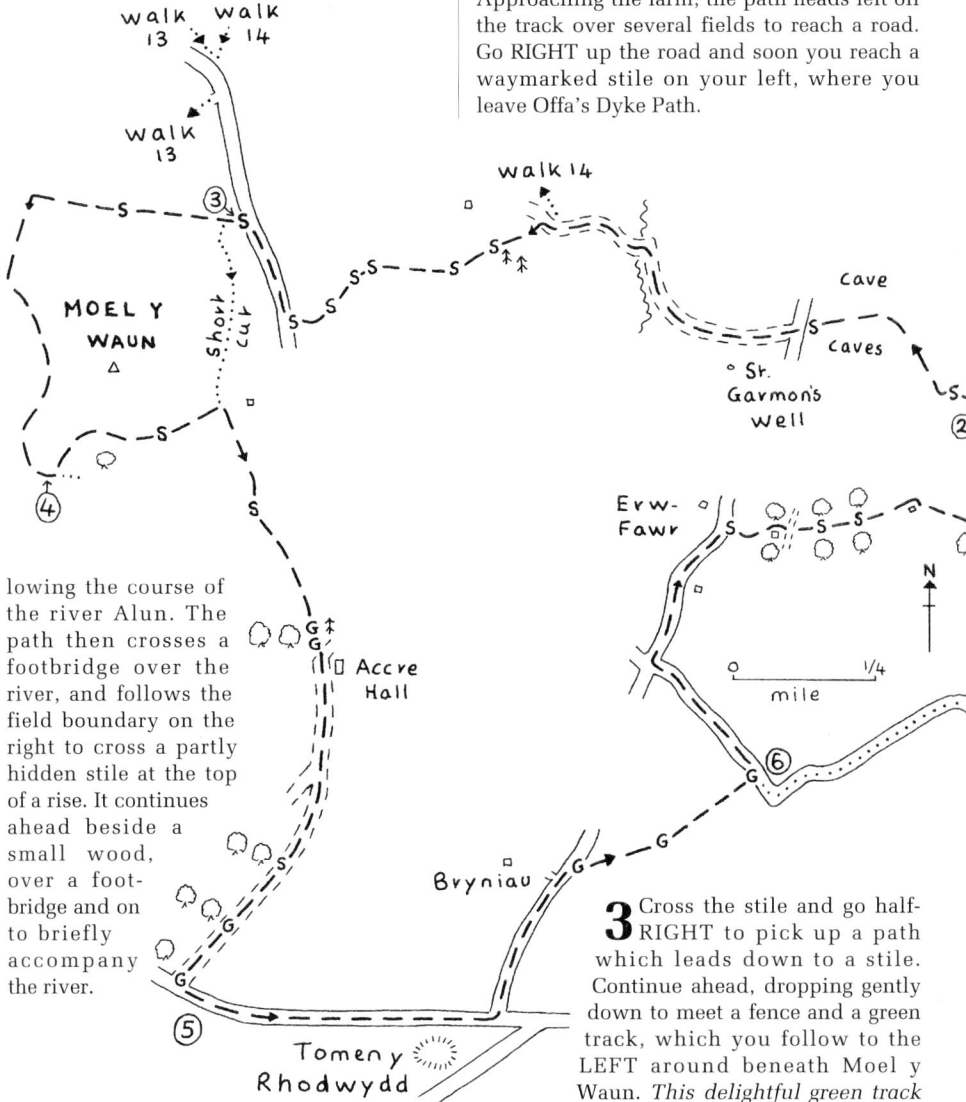

3 Cross the stile and go half-RIGHT to pick up a path which leads down to a stile. Continue ahead, dropping gently down to meet a fence and a green track, which you follow to the LEFT around beneath Moel y Waun. *This delightful green track*

WALK 15

Walk 15

THE ALUN VALLEY AND MOEL Y WAUN

DESCRIPTION This delightful 6½ mile walk from the old drovers village of Llandegla explores the tree-topped limestone country of the Alun valley and the open slopes of the southern Clwydians. The views are superb. It offers enjoyable walking amidst fine contrasting scenery, and provides an insight into an area rich in history. Highlights include an interesting church and a medieval fortress. Allow about 3½ hours.

START Church of St. Tegla, Llandegla. SJ 196524.

DIRECTIONS From the A525 Ruthin-Wrexham road, by the Crown Hotel, turn onto the A5104 road to Chester, and then left into the village of Llandegla. A car park is to be found on the right opposite the Memorial Hall, just before reaching the church.

---

offers panoramic views over the Vale of Clwyd towards the distant mountains of Snowdonia, the Berwyns and Llantisilio Mountain.

4 When the track bends down to the left, head LEFT up the slope above an area of gorse, aiming for a small aerial on the top of Moel y Waun. Swing RIGHT to pass through a gap in the fence and on up to cross over a stile on the shoulder of the hill. *Ahead are fine views over Llanarmon-yn-ial, Llandegla, and the moors beyond.* Continue ahead down the slope towards a house to a fence. Turn RIGHT and follow the line of an old field boundary to soon bear half-RIGHT to cross a stile, and on to pick up the boundary on your left, soon dropping down through two gates, and on along a tree-lined track behind *Accre Hall*. Keep on this main track to reach a road.

5 Follow the road LEFT to a junction. *Just beyond a 'Give-Way' sign, you will see on your right the distinctive shape of Tomen y Rhodwydd – one of the finest medieval motte and bailey castles in Wales, built in 1149 by Owain Gwynedd during his conquest of northern Powys. It occupies an important strategic position controlling the Nant-y-Garth pass through the Clwydians.* Turn LEFT on the B5431, and after passing the entrance to *Bryniau*, where *an ancient cutting stone tool originating from Penmaenmawr was found in 1922.* Go through the first gate on your right, and head half-LEFT to a gate, and continue straight on to a minor road.

6 *Here you have a choice.* Turning right will take you direct to Llandegla, but a more interesting route is to turn LEFT. At a junction, follow the road RIGHT, and just before the entrance to *Erw-fawr*, turn RIGHT over a stone stile alongside a gate. Go ahead, soon swinging LEFT and then RIGHT, past a corrugated shed to reach a cross-track. Go half-LEFT down on to a grassy shelf, and down through the trees to cross a stile ahead, then on half-LEFT to another stile. Continue half-LEFT, to soon follow a field boundary on your left. Just past a derelict cottage above you, turn RIGHT on to the limestone ridge. Go half-LEFT to find a hidden ladder stile in the prominent tree-clad ridge ahead. Continue slightly LEFT to gain more open pasture, and then ahead through a field gap and across a large field to a road. Follow this to the LEFT into Llandegla. *By the old bridge over the River Alun is the spot where drovers used to leave their animals. Close to the village lies St. Tegla's Holy Well, reputed to be the oldest healing well in Wales, famous for the cure of epilepsy until the early 19thC. Nearby is a large piece of sandstone, known locally as the 'Roman Stone'. It is of great antiquity, and is possibly the missing village cross.*

PRONUNCIATION

These basic points should help non-Welsh speakers

Welsh	English equivalent
c	always hard, as in **c**at
ch	as on the Scottish word lo**ch**
dd	as th in **th**en
f	as v in **v**ocal
ff	as f
g	always hard as in **g**ot
ll	no real equivalent. It is like 'th' in **th**en, but with an 'L' sound added to it, giving '**thlan**' for the pronunciation of the Welsh 'Llan'.

In Welsh the accent usually falls on the last-but-one syllable of a word.

KEY TO THE MAPS

- → Walk route and direction
- = Metalled road
- = = = Unsurfaced road
- ∞∞∞ Wall
- • • • • Footpath/route adjoining walk route
- ▬▬▬ Railway
- ～ River/stream & flow
- ↟ ۩ Trees
- ෆ Shrub/bracken/gorse
- G Gate
- S Stile
- F.B. Footbridge
- ⊻⊻ Viewpoint
- [P] Parking
- [T] Telephone
- [i] Tourist Information Centre

THE COUNTRY CODE

Enjoy the countryside and respect its life and work

Guard against all risk of fire

Leave gates *as you find them*

Keep your dogs under close control

Keep to public paths across farmland

Use gates and stiles to cross fences, hedges and walls

Leave livestock, crops and machinery alone

Take your litter home

Help to keep all water clean

Protect wildlife, plants and trees

Take special care on country roads

Make no unnecessary noise

Cover photographs: large - The Vale of Clwyd (walk 12), inset: Moel Famau (walks 8 & 10). Both by David Berry.
Illustrations: Morag Perrott

Created on a Macintosh, using Works, Freehand, Photoshop and QuarkXPress
Printed by WPG, Welshpool
First edition 1999. Revised November 2000.

ISBN: **1 902302 04 4**

Published by
Kittiwake 3 Glantwymyn Village Workshops, nr Machynlleth, Montgomeryshire SY20 8LY

© *Text & maps*: David Berry 1999
© *Illustrations*: Kittiwake 1999